CREATING COLOR

A Dyer's Handbook

Written and Illustrated by

Judy Anne Walter

Cooler By the Lake Publications

1989

Dedication

To Larry, my partner in love and laughter

Creating Color : A Dyer's Handbook

Copyright 1989   by Judy Anne Walter

Cover illustration: "Arrows, 3 Part Harmony" Copyright 1987 Judy Anne Walter

All of the information contained in this book is complete and accurate to the best of the author's knowledge. There is no guarantee connected with this information, nor does the publisher nor the author assume any liability associated with the use of the information.

Published by   Cooler By The Lake Publications
                P.O. Box 6149
                Evanston, IL 60204

Printed and bound in the United States of America.
ISBN# 0-9621871-0-0
Library of Congress Catalog Card Number 89-81114

Preface

Why dye fabric?

I raised this question to the first fiber artist I met who dyed her own fabric. She explained how this gave her any color she wanted. Since (it seemed to me) you could get every color in commercially dyed fabric, I wasn't impressed at the time.

As time went by and my designing abilities grew, her response made more and more sense. I could not get all the colors I wanted in commercial fabrics, especially those hard-to-find yellows and greens. There were times when I ran out of a color and wished I had a small fabric company in my basement. I also wanted fabric that came in light to dark values of a single color. These fabrics were difficult to find in stores.

I finally followed that fiber artist's advice. I took some workshops on dyeing with Procion MX series fiber reactive dyes (Elsa Sreenivasam, 1983; Jan Myers-Newbury, 1984). I corresponded with some dye houses, particularly PRO Chemical and Dye, Inc. My friends who were already dyeing fabric, Kathy McKeever and Caryl Fallert, encouraged me. And I started experimenting. I discovered that dyeing fabric was fun, easy, and rewarding! No matter how splotchy the fabrics were at first, I could find a use for them. (This could not be said for my earliest experiments with cooking.) The results lasted, unlike dyed Easter eggs. Lastly, by using Procion MX series dyes, the color in the fabric was permanent. This had not been my experience with household dyes. I could get rich intense colors that would not bleed or fade or eventually wash out.

Why another dyebook?

As I continued to work with Procion MX series dyes, I found that there was little literature that satisfied all my needs. I felt that I had to sift through a lot of information that was relevant to someone who wove or knit. Since the fabric I dye goes into my quilts, I wanted specific information for dyeing small amounts of fabric in an economic and efficient way that would give me the most intense colors possible. I also wanted a color mixing method that would enable me to reproduce colors I had previously dyed.

Through my search for more information, I learned to use the dyes more effectively and economically by not exceeding the manufacturer's recommendations. I developed the "Basic Concentrate System" to make both dye measuring and color mixing simpler. This allows me to reproduce colors easily, write color recipes more efficiently, and mix colors more effectively.

This book is the result of my exploration with Procion MX dyes. These dyes work on most natural fibers, but since wools require a different dyeing procedure, instruction for dyeing them will not be given.

I hope that this book will satisfy all your questions and encourage you to experiment on your own.

Acknowledgements

I would like to thank the following people for their assistance and support in developing this book:

my husband, Larry Bole

my parents, Fred and Dorothy Walter, who supplied me with a place to dye fabric

my friends, Judy Perry, Kathy McKeever, and Caryl Fallert, with whom I've had many conversations about dyeing

my students from Northwest Suburban Quilters Guild, Heritage Quilters, Dekalb Quilters, Prairie Star Quilt Guild, and at the Quilt Carlinville '87 and the Great Lakes Biennial 1988 conferences who helped me develop this material, with a special thanks to Lynn Rice, Millie Churbuck, Kathy Flink, and Lotus Phillips who asked the right questions at the right time

Don and Adele Wiener at PRO Chemical and Dye, Inc. for technical assistance

Jan Myers-Newbury and Elsa Sreenivasam, from whom I began learning about dyeing

Virginia Avery, Nancy Halpern, Carla Hassel, Maria McCormick-Snyder, Kathy McKeever, Jan Myers-Newbury, Judy Perry, Liz Porter, Ami Simms, and Don Wiener who read and commented on earlier versions of this book.

and a special thanks to Don Rechenbacher, Susan Clark, and Dwight Reinhardt at Chicago Computer Company, and Ty Bardi and Marla Ushkow at Kinko's in Evanston for technical assistance.

Creating Color: A Dyer's Handbook

Table of Contents

Preface iii

CHAPTER 1   Introduction: Where to Begin 1
CHAPTER 2.   Quickstart 3
CHAPTER 3.   Procion MX Dyes 5
CHAPTER 4.   Dye Safety 7
CHAPTER 5.   Setting up a Dyeing Area at Home 9
CHAPTER 6.   Dyeing Equipment 10
CHAPTER 7.   Dyebath Ingredients 15
CHAPTER 8.   Dye 24
CHAPTER 9.   Basic Concentrate System 37
CHAPTER 10. How to Dye 49
CHAPTER 11. Troubleshooting 54
CHAPTER 12. Record Keeping 56
CHAPTER 13. Basic Color Theory 59
CHAPTER 14. Color Mixing for Dyers 66
CHAPTER 15. Color Gradations 67
CHAPTER 16. Color Mixing with Color Gradations 73
CHAPTER 17. Dye Characteristics 90
CHAPTER 18. Frequently Asked Questions 92
CHAPTER 19. Washing Machine Dyeing 96
CHAPTER 20. Additional Projects 99
CHAPTER 21. Abbreviations and Equivalencies 112
CHAPTER 22. Dye Color Comparision Chart 113
CHAPTER 23. Suppliers 115
CHAPTER 24. Bibliography 116
CHAPTER 25. Glossary 117

Index 119

Charts

CHART 1. Dyebath Ingredient Summary for Quilt-cotton 19

CHART 2. Dyebath Ingredient Formula Summary 23

CHART 3. Dye Class Charts for Quilt-cotton 27

CHART 4. Dye Weight Classes .44

CHART 5. Basic Concentrate Charts for Quilt-cotton 45

CHART 6. Sample Color Recipe 58

CHART 7. Dye Recommendations. 61

CHART 8. Washing Machine Dyebath Ingredients 97

Projects

PROJECT 1. 3 Dyebaths. 35

PROJECT 2. Color Wheel (Dyebath by Dyebath). 62

PROJECT 3. Color Wheel (Basic Concentrate) 64

PROJECT 4. Simple Color Gradation Series. 71

PROJECT 5. Simple Two Color Gradation. 76

PROJECT 6. Gradation with a Constant 80

PROJECT 7. Same Quantity Gradation 84

PROJECT 8. One Up, One Down Gradation. 88

CHAPTER 1.

Introduction: Where to Begin

You've decided to dye your own fabrics or to learn more about using Procion MX series fiber reactive dyes. Here's how to get started!

Begin your dyeing adventure by ordering the catalogs from the various dye houses listed under Suppliers (Chapter 23) in this book and in the advertisements of fiber magazines. The chapters in this book on equipment (Chapter 6) and color theory (Chapter 13) will help you decide what dyes and equipment you want and what you may have to order by mail.

Prepare for your first dye session by reading through this book. You will find suggestions for which chapters should be read first in the Quickstart chapter. Many of the recommended chapters contain a quickstart guide within them. The Quickstart chapter also suggests several beginning projects, the equipment needed for them, and the relevant sections of the book to read for that project. Planning sheets for sample projects can be found at the end of the chapters on Dye (Chapter 8), Color Theory (Chapter 13), Color Gradations (Chapter 15), and in the chapter on "Color Mixing with Color Gradations" (Chapter 16). Additional projects can be found in Chapter 20.

Before your first dye session, **accumulate all your dyeing equipment**, using the checklist in Chapter 6. Plan how you will set up your dyeing area (Chapter 5). Be sure you understand how to use these dyes safely (Chapter 4).

During your first few dye sessions, only do a few dyebaths at a time, using small amounts of fabric. These sessions may go slowly (and your results may not be perfect), but they will familiarize you with the dyeing process. Also use this time to test the setup of your dyeing area and your equipment.

When you feel confident with fabric dyeing, increase the number of dyebaths you do in a single session. Don't do too many, or you will feel like the sorceror's apprentice! Run a Simple Color Gradation Series (Chapter 15) for every new dye you get. This takes six to eight dyepots. These color gradations provide information you will need for color mixing.

You may also want to take a dyeing class through an art center or a textile guild. If you would like to read more about fiber reactive dyes, I recommend the instruction sheets printed by the dye houses (Chapter 23) or the books mentioned in the bibliography (Chapter 24). You may further benefit by dyeing with a friend who already knows how to do it.

When you turn to other sources on fiber reactive dyes and dyeing, you will find that there is more than one way to dye with Procion MX dyes. All the information in this book has been tested in my own

1

own dyeing sessions and in the workshops I offer. I have provided the reasons for all the steps and procedures which I use.

Remember that dyeing fabric does take some practice. The more you do it, the better you will get. Even if you have been dyeing fabric for some time and are only adding some new techniques from this book to your dyeing routine, be prepared for an adjustment period. When you become comfortable with fabric dyeing, you should have discovered something that is very pleasurable and rewarding to do. Enjoy yourself!

CHAPTER 2.

Quickstart

This is a **quickstart**--a fast way to get into this book! Of course, I recommend that you read the entire book. But I am sure that there are a few of my readers who would like to read the least amount of literature possible and begin dyeing immediately!

There are some portions of the book **everyone** should read before they begin dyeing. But, after that, I will give recommended sections for different types of dyers and dyeing situations and suggest a project. Hopefully, there will be a quickstart situation that applies to you!

Everyone should read:

Chapter 4:	Dye Safety
Chapter 5:	Setting up a Dyeing Area at Home
Chapter 6:	Dyeing Equipment
Chapter 7:	Dyebath Ingredients
Chapter 8:	Dye
Chapter 10:	How to Dye
Chart 1:	Dyebath Ingredient Summary for Quilt-Cotton

For the fastest quickstart, I recommend that you use cotton broadcloth or muslin (what I call quilt-cotton), and use the sample projects throughout the book. If you do not use quilt-cotton, you will need to read the sections on calculating ingredients found in Chapter 7: Dyebath Ingredients and Chapter 8: Dye.

Situation #1. You are a brand new dyer. I recommend that you limit your first dye session to 3 dyepots. You should read in addition to the general chapters listed above:

Project #1: 3 Dyebaths (p. 35)

You will need 1-1/2 yards of quilting weight cotton and these dyes: PRO Blue 404, Red MX-5B, and Yellow MX-4G.

Situation #2. You are a brand new, adventurous dyer. You are prepared to dye a LOT of fabric on your first dye session. A Simple Color Gradation Series is a good beginning. You should read in addition to the general chapters mentioned above:

Project #4: Simple Color Gradation Series (p.71)
Chapter 9: Basic Concentrate System
Chapter 15: How to Do a Simple Color Gradation

You will need 3 yards of quilting weight cotton and Black MX-CWA dye.

Situation #3. You are a brand new, adventurous dyer who is interested in learning about colors. Here's how to dye a Color Wheel. You should read in addition to the general chapters mentioned above:

either:

> Project #2: Color Wheel
> (Dyebath by Dyebath) (p. 62)
> Chapter 12: Basic Color Theory

or:

> Project #3: Color Wheel
> (Basic Concentrate) (p.64)
> Chapter 9: Basic Concentrate
>   System
> Chapter 12: Basic Color Theory

The first set of readings will explain the Dyebath by Dyebath method of dye mixing; the second set will explain the Basic Concentrate method. You have a choice!

You will need 3 yards of quilting weight cotton and these dyes: PRO Blue 404, Red MX-5B, and Yellow MX-4G.

How did your fabric turn out? If it wasn't perfect, read Chapter 11 on troubleshooting.

Additional Projects can be found in Chapters 15, 16, and 20.

CHAPTER 3.

Procion MX Fiber-reactive Dyes

Imperial Chemical Industries, Ltd. (ICI) introduced Procion MX series fiber reactive dyes in 1956. They are synthetic dyes that react chemically with natural fibers, particularly vegetable fibers like cotton and linen. They are both colorfast and reasonably lightfast, so they will not bleed nor fade excessively. The dyes come in a full color range. In addition to exhaust dyeing, these dyes can be used for batiking, tie dyeing, painting, stamping, silk-screening, etc.

Procion MX dyes work best on viscose rayon, 100% mercerised cotton, 100% linen, 100% unmercerised cotton, linen and cotton blends. (Although rayon is considered a synthetic fiber because it is man-made, it is made of natural fibers. Viscose rayon is made from wood pulp. Other rayons are made from cotton by-products.) The dyes do not work on synthetic fibers at all. For the best results, the fabrics should have no sizing or other finishes. If you dye permanent press fabrics, expect to use more than the usual amount of dye. Be prepared that your fabric may not dye as dark as similarly dyed non-permanent press fabrics would.

Dyeing with Procion MX dyes requires only simple household-type equipment and easily obtainable materials. Ordinary table salt, water softener, and soda ash are the only additional chemicals needed.

It is helpful to have a brief picture of the chemical process that occurs during the dyeing session. (This section was prepared with the help of the book, *Synthetic Dyes for Natural Fibers* by Linda Knutsen (Interweave Press, Loveland Co, 1986), pp 31-33, 50-53.) This process can be broken down into three distinct phases.

The first phase is the **exhaust** phase. In preparation for this phase, dampened fabric is placed in a solution of water, dye, and salt. It will soak (with occasional rearrangings) in this solution for 15-20 minutes. During this time, the fabric adsorbs the dye with the assistance of the salt. (Adsorption is the assimilation of the dye onto the surface of the fiber by the surpression of the negative surface charges of the fiber.) Simply stated, the salt helps the dye stick to the fabric. The greater the amount of salt used, the higher the adsorption and the deeper the color will be.

The second phase is the **reactive** phase. At this time, the adsorbed dye is locked in the fabric so it will not wash off. The color becomes permanent. Adding a solution of dissolved soda ash to the dyebath raises the pH of the water. This allows the dye molecules to react chemically with the fiber molecules. It takes about an hour for this reaction to occur fully. The dye is now "set."

The third and last phase is the **scouring** stage. Because the dye reacts with the water (called hydrolization) as well as with the fiber, the fabric must be thoroughly rinsed in warm water to remove the soda ash and then scoured in hot water to remove all the excess salt and dye. The hydrolysed dye molecules stick to the fabric, but do not chemically react with it. If this excess dye is not removed, the fabric will bleed. Detergents, like Synthrapol, are designed to remove excess dye.

The Safe Dyer

CHAPTER 4.

Dye Safety

Procion MX series fiber reactive dyes are among the safest of all dyes available for home use. **The dyes are not toxic and contain no known carcinogens.** Occasionally, some people find they are allergic to the dyes. The primary health problems associated with these dyes have been respiratory ones. These usually have developed during prolonged exposure in an industrial environment. For more information, read the dye safety and information sheets for Procion MX series dyes. They are available from Cerulean Blue and PRO Chemical and Dye, Inc. (See Chapter 23.)

Do not work with dyes if you are pregnant. No tests have been done on them in regards to pregnancy. Because these are commercial dyes, it is unlikely that tests will be done in the foreseeable future.

To avoid ingesting the dye, safety equipment should be worn during your dye session. Wear a **face mask** for fine dust particles or a respirator while measuring the powdered dye in order to avoid breathing it. Plastic **safety goggles** will protect your eyes from airborn dye particles or splashed dye solutions.

The dye cannot "enter" your body through your pores. Nonetheless you should protect your skin. Wear **rubber gloves** to avoid prolonged skin contact with the dyebath. To avoid getting the fine powder in your hair and on your scalp,

you should cover your head with a scarf or a cap. After you are done dyeing, shower. Although these safety precautions may seem extreme and imposing, I believe using these dyes is much less risky than using many household products such as oven cleaner, drain opener, and insecticide.

Most of the precautions for using Procion MX dyes safely are a matter of common sense. The dyes are chemicals and should be treated with care. Obviously, **do not eat or drink any of the dyes or dye concentrates.** Nor should you eat or drink (or smoke, obviously) in the area where you are working with the powdered dye. Keep the dyes away from children and pets. Clean up spilled dry dye immediately with damp rags or sponges. Wash the dye-stained rag and sponges with your dyed fabric so they can be reused.

Here are some suggestions for handling the dyes safely. (1) Cover the surface of your measuring area with dampened sponge sheets (available in most housewares departments) to catch and absorb any spilled dye. (2) Rinse off or soak your measuring spoons in water immediately after use. (3) Only open one jar of dye at a time, and replace the lid immediately after measuring. (4) Wipe the outside of dye jars clean after each dyeing session with damp sponges or rags.

Plan your dyeing area with safety in mind. (See also Chapter 5.) The room where you do the dyeing should be well ventilated, but have no drafts from windows or air vents that will scatter the powdered dye. As a further safety precaution, you can make a **measuring chamber** to provide an enclosed measuring space in which to measure the powdered dye. Here are a few suggestions for measuring chambers:

(1) Line the inside of a large (i.e. 18" x 18" x 18") deep cardboard box with light colored vinyl adhesive shelving paper. Turn the box on its side so the opening to the box faces you. Place the jars of dye and the measuring equipment inside. With your arms inside the chamber, measure the dyes. Wipe the interior of the box clean after each use. The drawback to this simple method is the impaired visibility. You will not be able to see clearly what your hands are doing.

(2) You can make a more efficient measuring chamber from a cardboard box which has armholes cut on each side, and a removable clear acrylic plastic top. This is similar to the first suggestion except the chamber is closed on all four sides, and you can see what you are doing.

(3) If you can work comfortably at your laundry or utility sink, use it as a measuring chamber. Place a narrow sheet of plexiglass over the sink, leaving room for your arms on either side. The airborn dye will not be able to float higher than the glass. When you are finished, rinse the glass and the sink. **Do not use your kitchen sink as a measuring area.**

Do not use any utensil for both preparing food and measuring dyes. Because dyeing equipment looks like kitchen equipment, it should be labeled "for dyeing only" or marked in some fashion. Store it away from the kitchen and other food preparation areas.

Another important safety factor is the packaging for your dyes. Many dye houses now routinely package the dye in plastic jars. If you purchase dye which is sold in bags or envelopes, transfer it to plastic jars. If you order your dyes by mail, examine any shipping carton that contains dye before you open it. Although the dye houses pack their shipments securely, I would not open any carton that appears to have been damaged in shipping. Return these cartons to the dye house.

Procion MX series fiber reactive dyes are not available in a liquid form because they are too reactive. However, other types of fiber reactive dyes are. Using these dyes will simplify some of your safety precautions as the powdered dye has already been mixed into a concentrate. (There are some drawbacks to the liquid dyes. They are more expensive, and have a short shelf life.) You should still exercise common sense when using these products and follow all manufacturer's suggestions for safe use. Do not ingest them and avoid contact with your skin and eyes.

CHAPTER 5.

Setting Up a Dyeing Area at Home

Your dyeing area (which includes the measuring area) should be well lit, well ventilated, roomy, and close to your water source. Oftentimes a laundry area is perfect for this. Keep small children and pets out of the way while the dyeing process is going on. Make your dyeing area comfortable. Each batch of dyeing will keep you busy for about three hours.

As you set up your dyeing area, prepare in advance for your final cleanup. Place newspapers or plastic on the floor and work surfaces. Fill two buckets with water: one for rinsing your utensils, the other for rinsing your gloved hands. Set out another bucket to collect all the used measuring containers which accumulate during the dye session.

You will need a surface on which to work with the dye. This can be in a measuring chamber or a sink, or on a table, washer or dryer top, etc. (See Chapter 4.) If you are far from your water source, fill some plastic pitchers with warm water to use in your dye preparations.

Arrange the dyepots so they are easy to reach and won't tip over. If you elevate the dyepots, rather than placing them on the floor, your back will experience less fatigue. Picnic table benches, old coffee tables, chairs, or low patio tables are perfect for this. To make impromptu tables, place old doors or wide boards on overturned buckets, concrete blocks, etc.

Wear comfortable old clothing. This includes your underwear, socks, and shoes! (I have a coordinated dyeing ensemble which includes a splotchy T-shirt, splotchy underpants, and, of course, splotchy socks.) When you measure the dye, have an old scarf or cap to cover your hair. Remember to use a face mask for fine dust particles, protective safety goggles, and rubber gloves. Always rinse off your gloves before you remove them.

Consider dyeing fabric outside on a very nice day. I have found I can use water from the outside faucet for everything except the final rinsing, which should be done in hot water. It is not advisable to empty the used dyebath on your lawn. The salt contained in the dyebath attracts animals who will lick the grass that is contaminated with soda ash and spent dye powder.

Used dyebath solutions can be emptied into a sewer line or a septic system below surface. Contact your local water service for disposal advice if you are dyeing in an area that has wells and/or no sewer systems, or if you are disposing of more than 2 pounds of dye per week.

CHAPTER 6.

Dyeing Equipment

This dyeing equipment checklist and the detailed discussion which follows will help you collect your equipment. Many of the items can be obtained in a housewares department. They need not be recognizable brand names, and it need not all match. (In short, designer dyeware is not necessary!)

Dyeing Equipment Checklist

|_| Fabric

|_| Procion MX series fiber reactive dyes

|_| Soda ash

|_| Salt

|_| Calgon water softener (only if needed)

|_| Wide and shallow containers for dyepots

|_| Half gallon pitchers

|_| Measuring pitchers, beakers, 2 cup measures, measuring cups

|_| Measuring spoons

|_| 8 oz to 16 oz mixing containers

|_| Long handled stirring spoons

|_| Syringe pipettes (optional)

|_| Laboratory thermometer (optional)

|_| Scale

|_| Waterproof pen for coding fabrics (optional)

|_| Calculator, pen and paper

|_| Timer

|_| Paper towels, rags, sponges, sponge sheets, plastic sheeting

|_| Three buckets for holding rinse water, utensils, etc.

|_| Synthrapol detergent

|_| Washing machine

|_| Clothes dryer (optional)

|_| Fine dust particle face mask

|_| Rubber gloves

|_| Safety goggles

|_| Something to cover your hair

Dyeing Equipment

Fabric Use any fabric that is 100% cotton, linen, viscose rayon, silk, etc. It should not have any finishes. Prior to dyeing, prescour **all** fabrics in hot (140º F) water, using 1 teaspoon Synthrapol and 1 teaspoon soda ash per pound of fabric. See Chapter 7 for more information about fabric and Chapter 23 for some recommended fabric sources.

Dye Most dyers prefer to obtain their Procion MX series fiber reactive dyes by mail order in order to get the widest selection of colors and the most reasonable prices. The Suppliers section (Chapter 23) at the back of this book lists some dye houses. Check fiber and textile art magazines for the addresses of new companies. Try to buy dye that is distributed directly from Imperial Chemical Industries, Inc. (ICI) to the dye house and is sold in a pure, unadulterated form.

I usually buy my dye in 2 ounce jars. This amount should dye around six pounds of fabric, or 25 yards of quilting weight fabric a medium shade. In general, expect the yellow dyes to be used up the quickest, and the fuchsia dye, Fuchsia MX-8B, to go very slowly.

Soda ash This is also called sal soda, washing soda, sodium carbonate, dense soda ash, "pH up," and "dye activator." It is not the same as baking soda (sodium bicarbonate). Do not use the washing soda that is sold in the grocery stores if it contains bleach. All dyehouses carry soda ash. It can also be purchased in bulk from stores that sell swimming pool supplies or ceramic supplies.

Salt Use noniodized table salt, coarse salt, Kosher salt, or pickling salt. Do not use rock salt, sea salt, evaporated salt or iodized salt.

Water softener Only add water softener if your water is hard. You can use either Calgon water softener which is sold in grocery stores or the water softener (sodium hexametaphosphate) sold by dye houses. Fabrics dyed in hard water will be blotchy and have uneven coloration.

Dyepots The containers used as dyepots can be stainless steel, enamel, glass, or plastic. Do not use aluminum or cast iron because they react with the dye. Select the right sized container for the job. Use wide and shallow containers rather than tall and narrow because the fabric needs to spread out while it is dyeing. Five gallon buckets, dishpans, restaurant dish busing pans, laundry tubs, and new plastic kitty litter pans are ideal. You will need one dyepot for each color you dye during a dye session.

Dye large amounts of fabric in a small plastic wading pool, the bathtub, or in a washing machine. If you use your bathroom, be sure the bathtub has been freshly scrubbed. Move all the towels, bathmats, shower curtains, etc., out of the room. Although the dye does not stain porcelain, use cleanser and/or bleach to scrub any discoloration that may appear on older, worn tubs. Instructions for washing machine dyeing are given in Chapter 19. The instruction pamphlets from some dye houses also include this information.

Water pitchers You need one or two half gallon water pitchers to hold the water used for dissolving the dyes, measuring the dye concentrates, and filling the dyepots.

Measuring equipment There are several types of measuring equipment needed for measuring the liquid ingredients.

You need either a two cup measure, a one quart measuring pitcher, or a 1000 ml beaker in which to dissolve the dye or combine the dye concentrates which will be later added to the dyebath. The measure should have some head space between the top edge and the top measuring line.

If you are using Basic Concentrates, you also need a one quart pitcher or a 1000 ml beaker for each Basic Concentrate you mix during a dye session. Some dyehouses sell inexpensive plastic beakers.

After the Basic Concentrates have been mixed, they are measured with measuring cups into the two cup or one quart measure. You will need at least one set of measuring cups with these measures: 1 C, 1/2 C, 1/3 C, 1/4 C, 1/8 C. You can use cups for measuring either liquids or solids.

Measuring spoons Use these to measure the dry ingredients (dye, salt, soda, and water softener). You will need at least two sets, preferably with long handles. The sets should have these measures: 1 T, 1/2 T, 1 tsp, 1/2 tsp, 1/4 tsp, and 1/8 tsp.

Mixing containers Use 8 oz to 16 oz plastic containers for holding the premeasured ingredients which are added to the dyepots during the dye session. You need two containers for every dyepot. One set of containers holds the dry ingredients (the salt and the water softener). The other set holds the wet (the dissolved soda ash). As a result, all the ingredients for each dyepot can be measured in advance. Add them to the dyepots at the appropriate times.

Long handled stirring spoons Use these spoons to stir dye concentrates, dissolve salt, and dissolve soda. The spoons can be either stainless steel or plastic. Do not use wooden spoons as they will absorb the dye and eventually dry out.

Syringe pipettes (optional) When measuring less than 1/8 C of dye concentrate, use a plastic syringe pipette. Some dye houses carry these.

Laboratory thermometer (optional) Use this thermometer to check the temperature of your dyebath. If your dyebath cools too rapidly, your fabric will not dye evenly. Dye houses and scientific supply stores sell laboratory thermometers.

Scale The weight of your fabric determines the amounts of all the ingredients that make up the dyebath. You will need either a kitchen scale (that measures ounces and pounds), a counterbalance scale, or a tri-beam scale.

Waterproof pen (optional) Use this to mark your fabrics with a coded number, the dye formula, etc., before you dye them. A finepoint laundry marker works well.

Calculator (optional) When you determine the amounts of the ingredients you need for the dyebath, do your math on a calculator.

Timer You need a timer to remind you to rearrange the fabric in the dyepot every 5 to 10 minutes during the dyeing cycle. Do not use your kitchen timer because it will get dye on it. Purchase a lightweight spring timer that can be hung around your neck. By wearing the timer, I never miss a time to rearrange the fabric, and I don't forget to reset it.

Paper towels, sponge sheets, etc. You need a variety of materials for keeping your dyeing area clean: rags, paper towels, sponges, sponge sheets, etc. Use old newspapers or plastic sheeting on the floor.

Synthrapol Use this detergent to prescour your fabric before it is dyed, and to wash it immediately after it is dyed. This economical detergent removes any excess dye and any chemicals that may be in your fabric, rather than the food stains and greasy oily dirt your household detergent treats. All dye houses carry Synthrapol.

Washer and dryer Use your washing machine both to scour the fabric prior to dyeing and to get the excess dye out of the newly dyed fabric. The fabric may be either line or machine dried. The dye will not stain either appliance.

Extra buckets Have at least three extra buckets for holding rinse water for your gloved hands and the utensils, and for holding the used utensils. Also use them to store your dyeing equipment and dyes.

Dyer's wardrobe *Do not use dyes if you do not take protective safety measures.* Remember to wear **rubber gloves** at all times. Wear a **face mask** (for fine dust particles), **safety goggles**, and a head covering while you are measuring the powdered dye. Face masks and long rubber gloves are available from all dye houses. If you feel like you are part of the clean-up crew for a minor nuclear disaster, you are probably wearing the right wardrobe. Remember to wear clothing (including underwear, socks, and shoes) that can get stained or wet.

CHAPTER 7.

Dyebath Ingredients

The dyebath contains dye, salt, water softener, water, soda ash, and the fabric to be dyed. Before I begin dyeing, I determine the amounts of each of these ingredients. The dyebath ingredient formulas found in this book are applicable to any type, weight, or amount of fabric that can be dyed with Procion MX series dyes.

I do most of the calculations for the amounts of dyebath ingredient with the U.S. measurement system, but occasionally the smaller units of measurement found in the metric system are necessary. At these times, I do the calculation in metric, and then convert the results to the U.S. system. (If you would like more information about the use of the metric system in dyeing, see the bibliography in Chapter 24.) In some places, I have consistently rounded off the numbers in order to make the math easier to follow. These places are indicated. All of the ingredient measuring can be done with household equipment.

Because I realise some of my readers would like to dye something right away and read about formulas later, I have included a **quickstart** chart (Chart 1) in this chapter. It gives the dyebath ingredient amounts for working with cotton broadcloth or muslin or other fabrics often used in quiltmaking. These are medium-weight fabrics which standardly weigh four yards to the pound. I call this type of fabric, "**quilt-cotton.**"

The discussions in this chapter occur in this order: (1) a brief discussion of each ingredient, (2) a **quickstart** chart for dyeing with quilt-cotton, and (3) how to calculate the amounts of dye ingredients. A summary chart (Chart 2) of the ingredient formulas follows these discussions. The next chapter covers measuring dyes.

Fabric

For best results, only use natural fiber fabrics that have no sizing or finishes. Prescour all fabrics in hot (140º F) water prior to dyeing to remove all chemical residues that may be left in the fabric. To prescour, use 1 teaspoon of soda ash and 1 teaspoon of Synthrapol for every pound of fabric you place in your washing machine.

Before dyeing, weigh the dry fabric for each dyebath separately. Do not skip this step because the weight of the fabric to be dyed determines the amounts of **all** other ingredients for that dyebath. Use a kitchen scale or a counterbalance scale (or even, as a friend of mine does, the produce scale at the supermarket). The scale should be accurate and able to weigh both pounds and ounces.

Sample Fabric Weights

Here are some samples of diferent fabrics and their weights for a piece that is 36" x 45". Add your own fabrics to this list.

Cotton Batiste	(Testfabrics #435)	81 gm
Cotton Calico		92 gm
Cotton Printcloth	(Testfabrics #400m)	112 gm
Cotton Pima Broadcloth	(Cerulean Blue)	120 gm
Cotton Muslin	(Ecology Cloth and R & Z)	135 gm
Cotton Sateen	(Testfabrics #428)	183 gm
Tablecloth Fabric	(Testfabrics #455)	245 gm
Cotton Velveteen	(Testfabrics #448)	260 gm
Spun Viscose Rayon Challis	(Cerulean Blue)	160 gm
Silk		92 gm
Silk Noil		198 gm
Silk Boucle		251 gm

To help you see the importance of weighing your fabric, some sample weights of different types of fabric are listed on the previous page. Each piece of fabric is 36" by 45". The supplier which carries the fabric or the brand I used in this sampling is stated when known. All of the listed fabrics have the average weight for fabrics of their type. The wide variation in their weights should indicate the need for actually weighing the fabric.

Water

Always measure the water used in the dyebath. The amount of water used relates directly to the amount of fabric dyed.

The manufacturers of Procion MX series dyes recommend using 2-1/2 gallons of water to dye one pound of fiber. This relationship between water and fiber is expressed as a 20:1 ratio of water weight to fabric weight.

Example Four yards of quilt-cotton would be dyed in 2-1/2 gallons of water because four yards of quilt-cotton weigh one pound and 2-1/2 gallons weigh 20 pounds.

The amounts of water needed for other common amounts of quilt-cotton are listed in Chart 1. Examples of how to determine the amount of water for other amounts of fabric will follow Chart 1.

The amount of water expressed by this ratio is the **total** amount of water for your dyebath. This includes the water used for dissolving and mixing the dyebath ingredients. **Any amounts of water used to prepare the other dyebath ingredients should be subtracted from the total amount of water.** This water is added to the dyebath later with the dissolved ingredient. Chart 1 contains recommendations on how to subdivide the water when dyeing quilt-cotton.

Water Softener

Hard water contains minerals that impede the dyeing process. Fabrics dyed in hard water are blotchy and have uneven coloration. If your water is hard, you will need to add water softener. Use either Calgon water softener or the water softeners sold by the dye houses.

If you are not sure if your water is hard, either contact the local water service, or run this test. Do two dyebaths that are identical in amounts of water, chemicals (including dye), and fabric. In one dyebath use distilled water. In the other use your tap water. Do not add any water softener to these test batches. If the fabric from the dyepot that used the household water is splotchy and unevenly colored when compared to the fabric from the dyepot with the distilled water, add the water softener to your dyebaths from now on.

Salt

The dyebath contains salt to make the fabric adsorb more dye. It is dissolved in the dyebath at the beginning of the dye session.

The amount of salt used affects the depth of the color being dyed. Consequentely, there are some dyeing situations when the amount of salt is adjusted. These cases are discussed in the next section in conjunction with soda ash.

Soda Ash

The soda ash raises the water's pH, which allows the dye and fabric molecules to react chemically to each other. Soda ash is also called sodium carbonate, washing soda, sal soda, "pH up" and "dye activator."

Dissolve the soda ash in a measured amount of hot (140º F) water before adding it to the dyebath. As before, the amount of water used to dissolve the soda ash is part of the total amount of water used for the dyebath. It has been subtracted from the total amount of water needed for the dyebath, and is added to the dyebath with the dissolved soda ash.

The amounts of both the soda ash and salt can be adjusted depending on the depth of color being dyed. These are the few times when I adjust the soda and salt: (1) the amount of salt can be cut in half when dyeing very light colors, (2) the amount of salt and/or soda ash can be doubled for very dark or intense colors like navy blue and black. Experiment to see how this affects your results.

Quickstart for Dyebath Ingredients

If you are using quilt-cotton, the following chart provides you with the amounts of water, water softener, salt, and soda ash you will need for dyeing 1/4, 1/2, 1, or 4 yards of this fabric type. If you are using an amount of quilt-cotton that is not on the chart, the chart can still help you determine it. For example, for 3 yards of fabric, multiply all the ingredients listed at 1 yard by 3.

If you are not using quilt-cotton, you will find the discussion of how to determine the amounts of dyebath ingredients after the chart.

18

CHART 1

Dyebath Ingredient Summary for Quilt-cotton

CHART 1: DYE BATH INGREDIENT SUMMARY FOR QUILT- COTTON

QUILT-COTTON	WATER*	SALT **	SOFTENER	SODA ASH**
4 YARD	2-1/2 gal, divided	I-l/2 C	3 T	6 T
1 YARD	2-1/2 qt, divided	3/8 C	1 T	1-1/2 T
1/2 YARD	1-1/4 qt, divided	3 T	1 tsp	2-1/4 tsp
1/4 YARD	2-1/2 C, divided	1-1/2 T	1/2 tsp	1 tsp

* HOW TO DIVIDE WATER FOR EACH DYEBATH

QUILT-COTTON	DISSOLVE SALT AND SOFTENER	DISSOLVE SODA	DISSOLVE DYE	TOTAL
4 YARDS	2 gal & 3 C	1 C	4 C	2-1/2 gal
1 YARD	7 C	1 C	2 C	2-1/2 qt
1/2 YARD	2 C	1 C	2 C	5 C
1/4 YARD	1/4 C	1/4 C	2 C	2-1/4 C

** EXCEPTIONS FOR AMOUNTS OF SALT AND SODA ASH:

Halve the amount of salt for very light hues
Double the amount of salt for dark hues
Double the amount of salt and soda for very dark hues

Calculating the Amount of Water

If the fabric you are dyeing is not covered by Chart 1, you need to figure the amount of water based on the weight of that fabric. Follow these three steps:

Step 1: Weigh the dry fabric.

Step 2: Multiply the weight of the fabric (in ounces) by 20. This is the weight of the water in ounces.

Step 3: Convert the weight of the water to a volume measurement like quarts or gallons. To do this, divide the weight of the water by the weight (in ounces) of either a gallon, a quart, or a pint. Use this information to do so:

One gallon of water weighs 8 lbs, or 128 oz
One quart of water weighs 2 lbs, or 32 oz
One pint of water weighs 1 lb, or 16 oz

The above steps can be expressed as a formula:

$$\frac{\text{Fabric wt} \times 20}{\text{(in oz)}} = \frac{\text{wt of water (in oz)}}{128 \text{ (wt in oz of one gal)}} = \text{\# of gal}$$

If you are using a small amount of fabric, divide the weight of the water by either 32 (the weight of one quart) or 16 (the weight of one pint.) This is the amount of water you need in quarts or pints.

Example You have 1 yard of gauzy fabric which weighs 3 ounces. Using the formula above:

$$3 \text{ oz} \times 20 = \frac{60 \text{ oz}}{32 \text{ oz}} = 1\text{qt} + 28 \text{ oz water}$$

Example You have 6 yards of fabric which weigh 2-1/2 pounds, or 40 ounces. Using the formula above:

$$40 \text{ oz} \times 20 = \frac{800 \text{ oz}}{128 \text{ oz}} = 6.25 \text{ gal}$$

This is the equivalent of 6 gallons and 1 quart of water, or 25 quarts.

Calculating the Amount of Salt

The weight of the salt should be equal to the weight of the fabric. One cup of salt weighs 10 ounces. For four yards of quilt-cotton which weigh 16 ounces, you would add 16 ounces of salt, or roughly one and a half cups.

Example You have one yard of fabric which weighs 3 ounces. You will need 3 ounces of salt, or roughly one third of a cup.

Example You have 6 yards of fabric which weigh 2-1/2 pounds, or 40 ounces. You will need 40 ounces of salt, or 2-1/2 cups.

Calculating the Amount of Water Softener

Use one teaspoon of water softener for every quart of water in your dyebath. Increase this amount if your water is very hard.

Example You are dyeing one yard of fabric which weighs 3 ounces in 1 quart, 28 ounces of water. You would use 1-7/8 teaspoon of water softener.

Example You are dyeing 6 yards of fabric which weigh 2-1/2 pounds in 6-1/4 gallons of water. This is 25 quarts. Add 25 teaspoons, or 8 tablespoons and 1 teaspoon of water softener to your dyebath.

Calculating the Amount of Soda Ash

The recommended amount of soda ash is 10% of the weight of the fabric. Metric measurements are the easiest to use when determining this amount. One pound of fabric weighs 453.6 grams. For math convenience, this will be rounded down throughout the book to 450 grams. Ten percent of 450 grams is 45 grams. One tablespoon of soda ash weighs 9 grams. Dividing 45 by 9 gives us 5 tablespoons of soda ash. Use 5 tablespoons of soda ash for every pound of fabric to be dyed.

Example You are dyeing one yard of fabric which weighs 3 ounces.

Step 1: Convert this weight to grams by multiplying the fabric weight (in ounces) by the number of grams in one ounce. One ounce weighs 28.53 grams, or (rounded off) 28.5 grams.

$$3 \times 28.5 = 85.5 \text{ gms fabric}$$

Step 2: Multiply this weight by 10% (0.10) to get the recommended amount of soda ash.

$$85.5 \times 0.10 = 8.55 \text{ gms, rounded off to } 8.5 \text{ gms soda ash}$$

Step 3: One teaspoon of soda ash weighs 3 grams. To determine how many teaspoons of soda ash are in 8.5 grams, divide by 3.

$$8.5 \div 3 = 2.8 \text{ tsp soda ash}$$

You need 2.8 teaspoons of soda ash. Since there are 3 teaspoons to a tablespoon, this is a scant tablespoon full.

Example You are dyeing 6 yards of fabric which weigh 2-1/2 pounds. Since the weight of the fabric is over one pound, multiply the weight of the fabric by the number of grams in a pound. This is 450, rounded down from 453.6.

$$2.5 \times 450 = 1125 \text{ gms fabric}$$

$$1125 \times 0.10 = 112.5 \text{ gms soda ash}$$

$$112.5 \div 3 = 37.5 \text{ tsps soda ash}$$

$$37.5 \div 3 = 12.5 \text{ T soda ash}$$

You need 112.5 grams of soda ash, or 12-1/2 tablespoons.

Use the amounts of all of these ingredients that give the best results. I occasionally round the figures off in order to simplify my measuring, as can be seen for the amounts of soda ash listed in Chart 1. Do not change the water weight to fabric weight ratio unless it is absolutely necessary. If you change it, the quantities of all other ingredients will also change.

Dyebath Ingredients

22

CHART 2

Dyebath Ingredient Formula Summary

CHART 2: DYEBATH INGREDIENT FORMULA SUMMARY

WATER Fabric Wt x 20 $= \dfrac{\text{wt of water (in oz)}}{128 \text{ (wt in oz of 1 gal)}} =$ number of gal
(in oz)

WATER SOFTENER 1 tsp per quart of water

SALT 100% x fabric wt

SODA ASH 10% x fabric wt

CHAPTER 8.

Dye

The last dyebath ingredient is the dye itself. Although the question, "How much dye do I need to dye this piece of fabric?", appears to be simple, there are a number of different factors to consider in answering it. These are discussed in the opening general introduction on dye. Measuring dye and calculating how much dye to use will also be discussed.

For those readers who want a **quickstart**, begin reading with the section entitled, "How to Measure Dye." Then use Chart 3 which provides information on dye amounts for dyeing quilt-cotton.

Introduction

The amount of dye you need depends primarily on two factors:

the weight of the fabric, and

the lightness or darkness (value) of the color you wish to dye.

The relationship between fabric weight and color intensity is described by the relationship of the dye weight to the fabric weight, where the **dye weight** is a **percentage of** the **weight** of the **fabric**, abbreviated %owf. In the example below, the number of grams in one pound has been rounded down to 450.

Example   4.0% of 1 lb (450 gm)
= 0.04 x 450 gm
= 18 gm dye

Most dyes achieve their deepest shades at **8%owf**. A few dyes, such as the bright yellows and turquoise, do not deepen above 4%owf. Lighter values of all colors use smaller amounts of dye. A pale hue could take an amount that weighs 0.125%owf.

Working with Dye

Dye may be measured in two ways: measured by the spoonful, or weighed on a gram scale, using either a counterbalance or tribeam scale. Weighing the dye is the more precise way to measure the dye. Because the small differences that arise from measuring dye by the spoonful are usually not apparent to the home dyer, I prefer to measure my dyes by the spoonful. In so doing I lessen my contact with the powdered dyes by measuring them directly into water, rather than measuring them on a scale and then dissolving them.

When dyes are measured, rather than weighed, the density of the dye must be considered. An equal weight of two dyes may not have the same measurement by the spoonful. Some dyes have a very fine consistency, others are very "fluffy." These differences will affect your measurement.

In order to simplify my dye measuring and still take into account the differences in dye density, I looked for some means of organizing my dyes by their densities. I measured out 18 grams of each of my dyes on a tribeam scale, keeping track of how many teaspoons and fractions of teaspoons of dye this was. I chose 18 grams as my base number because it (rounded off) is the number of grams of dye that equals 4% of the weight of one pound. After examining my results, I organized the information into six different weight classes.

Using the Dye Weight Class Chart (CHART 3.A-F)

The following chart lists each weight class of dye and the amounts of dye needed for certain color strengths for certain amounts of quilt-cotton. This information is subject to change. A dye may occasionally change from one weight class to another, depending on how the dyes are composed at the factory.

When you are determining how much dye you need to dye a piece of quilt-cotton, first look for your dye on this chart. Then find the depth of color you wish to dye your fabric. Remember the labels on the left side of the charts (dark, deep, etc.) are only suggestions for the color depth these amounts usually achieve. For example, a bright yellow dye will get more intense, but it will not get darker.

Lastly, find the amount of dye you would need for your amount of quilt-cotton. You will notice immediately that the fractions on the chart go as low as sixteenths and thirty-seconds of a

teaspoon. When a fraction gets smaller than that, I have placed an asterisk (*). How to handle these small amounts of dye powder will be discussed in the section, "How to Measure Dye," later in this chapter.

If your dye is not listed here or you suspect the factory has changed the composition of the dye, you have several options:

(1) Look at the Dye Color Comparison Chart in Chapter 22 for another dye with the same MX number that is on the chart.

Example You purchased the dye labeled "Cool Red" from Fabdec. It is not listed on the chart in this chapter. On the Dye Color Comparison Chart in Chapter 22, you will see that Cool Red MX-8B is also called PRO Red 308 MX-8B. This dye is listed under Class I (Chart 3.A). Add your dye to the Class I list.

(2) Look at the amount of dye in the jar and/or the size of the jar being used. Use the information from previously examined dyes to help you approximate the weight of the new dye.

Example You have purchased 2 ounce jars of Cerulean Blue MX-G and Turquoise MX-G. They were packaged in jars twice the size of the two ounce jars the other dyes you ordered came in. Use the Class VI section of Chart 3 to measure your dyes.

(3) For your first dyebath with this new dye, dye three pieces of fabric using the measurements for the 8%owf, 4%owf, and 2%owf stengths from the Class III weight class. This is the weight class for most dyes. Then, compare your fabric with the dye chart from the dye house where you buy your dye. You should be able to match the color on the color chart (the chart should indicate the strength at which that color was dyed). If your fabric is too light, use a higher weight class (Classes IV, V, or VI). If all three fabrics are the same color, use a lower weight class (Classes I or II).

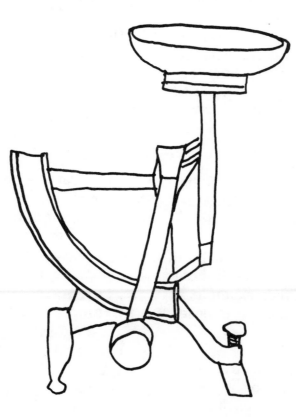

Counterbalance Scale

CHART 3.A

Class I Dyes

A **CLASS I DYE** is very dense in volume.

18 grams of powdered dye measures 3-1/2 to 4-1/4 tsp, or an average of 4 tsp.
One teaspoon of powdered dye weighs approximately 4.5 gms.

CHART 3.A: CLASS I DYE CHART FOR QUILT-COTTON				
HUE VALUE	**4 YARDS**	**1 YARD**	**1/2 YARD**	**1/4 YARD**
DARK (8%owf)	8 tsp dye	2 tsp dye	1 tsp dye	1/2 tsp dye
DEEP (4%owf)	4 tsp dye	1 tsp dye	1/2 tsp dye	1/4 tsp dye
MEDIUM (2%owf)	2 tsp dye	1/2 tsp dye	1/4 tsp dye	1/8 tsp dye
MED.LIGHT(1%owf)	1 tsp dye	1/4 tsp dye	1/8 tsp dye	(1/16 tsp dye)
LIGHT (0.5%owf)	1/2 tsp dye	1/8 tsp dye	(1/16 tsp dye)	(1/32 tsp dye)
VERY LT(0.25%owf)	1/4 tsp dye	(1/16 tsp dye)	(1/32 tsp dye)	*
PALE (0.125%owf)	1/8 tsp dye	(1/32 tsp dye)	*	*
CLASS I DYES				

PRO Fuchsia 308 MX-8B

CHART 3.B

Class II Dyes

A **CLASS II DYE** is moderately dense in volume.

18 grams of powdered dye measures 4-1/2 - 5-1/2 tsp, or an average of 5 tsp.
One teaspoon of powdered dye weighs approximately 3.5 gms.

CHART 3.B: CLASS II DYE CHART FOR QUILT-COTTON

HUE VALUE	4 YARDS	1 YARD	1/2 YARD	1/4 YARD
DARK (8%owf)	10 tsp dye	2-1/2 tsp dye	1-1/4 tsp dye	5/8 tsp dye
DEEP (4%owf)	5 tsp dye	1-1/4 tsp dye	5/8 tsp dye	(5/16 tsp dye)
MEDIUM (2%owf)	2-1/2 tsp dye	5/8 tsp dye	(5/16 tsp dye)	(5/32 tsp dye)
MED.LIGHT(1%owf)	1-1/4 tsp dye	(5/16 tsp dye)	(5/32 tsp dye)	*
LIGHT (0.5%owf)	5/8 tsp dye	(5/32 tsp dye)	*	*
VERY LT(0.25%owf)	(5/16 tsp dye)	*	*	*
PALE (0.125%owf)	(5/32 tsp dye)	*	*	*

CLASS II DYES

PRO Yellow MX-4G
Cerulean Blue MX-G conc (Cer. Blue)
PRO Cobalt Blue 406 MX-G conc (pre-1988)

PRO Blue 400 MX-R
B/F #2 Bright Yellow MX-4G
B/F #25 Turquoise MX-G

CHART 3.C

Class III Dyes

A **CLASS III DYE** has "average" density.

18 grams of powdered dye measures 6 tsp.
One teaspoon of powdered dye weighs approximately 3 gms.

CHART 3.C: CLASS III DYE CHART FOR QUILT-COTTON				
HUE VALUE	**4 YARDS**	**1 YARD**	**1/2 YARD**	**1/4 YARD**
DARK (8% owf)	12 tsp dye	3 tsp dye	1-1/2 tsp dye	3/4 tsp dye
DEEP (4% owf)	6 tsp dye	1-1/2 tsp dye	3/4 tsp dye	3/8 tsp dye
MEDIUM (2% owf)	3 tsp dye	3/4 tsp dye	3/8 tsp dye	(3/16 tsp dye)
MED. LIGHT (1% owf)	1-1/2 tsp dye	3/8 tsp dye	(3/16 tsp dye)	(3/32 tsp dye)
LIGHT (0.5% owf)	3/4 tsp dye	(3/16 tsp dye)	(3/32 tsp dye)	*
VERY LT (0.25% owf)	3/8 tsp dye	(3/32 tsp dye)	*	*
PALE (0.125% owf)	(3/16 tsp dye)	*	*	*

CLASS III DYES

PRO Yellow 108 MX-8G
PRO Orange 202 MX-2R
PRO Red 305 MX-5B
PRO Blue 404
PRO Chino 500
PRO Brown 505 MX-5BR
PRO Black 600 MX-CWA
PRO Grey 601
PRO Green 703 MX-C3BA

B/F #14 Coral
B/F #19A Lilac
B/F #21 Teal Blue
B/F #28 Blue Green MX-CBA
B/F #30 Emerald Green
B/F #32 Olive Drab
B/F #37 Bronze
B/F #38 Khaki
Red MX-GBA (Earth Guild)

CHART 3.D

Class IV Dyes

A **CLASS IV DYE** has medium-light density.

18 grams of powdered dye measures 6-3/4 - 7-1/2 tsp, or an average of 7 tsp.
One teaspoon of powdered dye weighs approximately 2.5 gms.

CHART 3.D: CLASS IV DYE CHART FOR QUILT-COTTON				
HUE VALUE	**4 YARDS**	**1 YARD**	**1/2 YARD**	**1/4 YARD**
DARK (8%owf)	14 tsp dye	3-1/2 tsp dye	1-3/4 tsp dye	7/8 tsp dye
DEEP (4%owf)	7 tsp dye	1-3/4 tsp dye	7/8 tsp dye	(7/16 tsp dye)
MEDIUM (2%owf)	3-1/2 tsp dye	7/8 tsp dye	(7/16 tsp dye)	(7/32 tsp dye)
MED.LIGHT(1%owf)	1-3/4 tsp dye	(7/16 tsp dye)	(7/32 tsp dye)	*
LIGHT (0.5%owf)	7/8 tsp dye	(7/32 tsp dye)	*	*
VERY LT(0.25%owf)	(7/16 tsp dye)	*	*	*
PALE (0.125%owf)	(7/32 tsp dye)	*	*	*
CLASS IV DYES				
PRO Black 602		PRO Purple 804		

CHART 3.E

Class V Dyes

A **CLASS V DYE** has a light composition.

18 grams of powdered dye measures 7-3/4 - 8-1/2 tsp, or an average of 8 tsp.
One teaspoon of powdered dye weighs approximately 2.25 gms.

CHART 3.E: CLASS V DYE CHART FOR QUILT-COTTON

HUE VALUE	4 YARDS	1 YARD	1/2 YARD	1/4 YARD
DARK (8%owf)	16 tsp dye	4 tsp dye	2 tsp dye	1 tsp dye
DEEP (4%owf)	8 tsp dye	2 tsp dye	1 tsp dye	1/2 tsp dye
MEDIUM (2%owf)	4 tsp dye	1 tsp dye	1/2 tsp dye	1/4 tsp dye
MED.LIGHT(1%owf)	2 tsp dye	1/2 tsp dye	1/4 tsp dye	1/8 tsp dye
LIGHT (0.5%owf)	1 tsp dye	1/4 tsp dye	1/8 tsp dye	(1/16 tsp dye)
VERY LT(0.25%owf)	1/2 tsp dye	1/8 tsp dye	(1/16 tsp dye)	(1/32 tsp dye)
PALE (0.125%owf)	1/4 tsp dye	(1/16 tsp dye)	(1/32 tsp dye)	*

CLASS V DYES

PRO Olive 708   PRO Yellow MX-GR

CHART 3.F

Class VI Dyes

A **CLASS VI DYE** has very light composition.

18 grams of powdered dye measures 8-3/4 - 9-1/2 tsp, or an average of 9 tsp.
One teaspoon of powdered dye weighs approximately 2 gms.

CHART 3.F: CLASS VI DYE CHART FOR QUILT-COTTON				
HUE VALUE	**4 YARDS**	**1 YARD**	**1/2 YARD**	**1/4 YARD**
DARK (8%owf)	18 tsp dye	4-1/2 tsp dye	2-1/4 tsp dye	1-1/8 tsp dye
DEEP (4%owf)	9 tsp dye	2-1/4 tsp dye	1-1/8 tsp dye	(9/16 tsp dye)
MEDIUM (2%owf)	4-1/2 tsp dye	1-1/8 tsp dye	(9/16 tsp dye)	(9/32 tsp dye)
MED.LIGHT(1%owf)	2-1/4 tsp dye	(9/16 tsp dye)	(9/32 tsp dye)	*
LIGHT (0.5%owf)	1-1/8 tsp dye	(9/32 tsp dye)	*	*
VERY LT(0.25%owf)	(9/16 tsp dye)	*	*	*
PALE (0.125%owf)	(9/32 tsp dye)	*	*	*

CLASS VI DYES

PRO Navy 420c MX-RB 150%   B/F #4 Deep Yellow MX-3RA
Midnight Blue MX-RB (Cer. Blue)   B/F #22 Cobalt Blue

Chart 5 (found in Chapter 9) repeats the information found in Chart 3, but organizes it differently. The dyes are listed there by their weight class for using them in concentrates when dyeing quilt-cotton. Each section of Chart 5 is for a different amount of quilt-cotton.

How to Measure Dye

There are two methods for preparing the dye. In one method, the dye for each dyebath is measured and dissolved **individually**. This chapter covers this method, the "Dyebath by Dyebath Method", in depth. With the other method, the "Basic Concentrate Method", the amount of each dye needed for the dye session is measured and dissolved **collectively**. It is then divided among the dyepots. Measure dyes with this method when they are used in several different dyebaths during a single dye session, or over a period of up to 3-5 days. I will discuss this method in Chapter 9 when I introduce the "Basic Concentrate System."

Procion MX series fiber reactive dyes are sold in a very concentrated powdered form. In most cases, only small amounts of the dye powder are necessary. To insure that the dye is thoroughly mixed into the dyebath, always prepare it by dissolving it in warm water.

Follow this procedure to prepare the dye. **Put on your rubber gloves, face mask, and safety goggles.** Sprinkle the powdered dye into a measured amount of warm water (not over 110º F). Then stir until the dye is dissolved. **Be careful not to get the powdered dye airborn.** Add this dissolved dye to the dyebath at the appropriate time.

The amount of water used to dissolve the dye is part of the water needed for the dyebath. In order to make my dye mixing more uniform, I try to use the same amount of water for dissolving the dye. This will have some variance, depending on the weight of the fabric. When I am dyeing one pound or more, I use **four** cups of water to dissolve the dye. If I am dyeing less than one pound, I use **two** cups. In this case, I subtract two cups from the total amount of dyebath water every time I dye less than one pound of fabric. In the case of one pound or more of fabric I subtract four cups from the total amount of dyebath water I need. This water is used to dissolve the dye, and is then added to the dyepot. (See Chart 1.)

The following discussion will be written as if I were dyeing less than one pound of fabric and dissolving my dye in 2 cups of water. This is for the sake of convenience. If you are dyeing over one pound of fabric, remember to use four cups for dissolving dye. The dye is soluble only up to 6 teaspoons per cup. In most dyeing situations, the amounts of dye needed for one pound or more of fabric will not properly dissolve in two cups of water.

Sometimes the amount of dye you need is too small for you to measure directly. This happens frequently on Chart 3. In these cases, go upwards in the chart to find an amount you can measure. Usually this is one or two lines above. Predissolve this amount of dye into one cup of warm water. Use a portion of this dissolved dye in place of the measured powdered dye.

Example You want to dye one half yard of fabric a light color, using PRO Fuchsia MX-8B. This is a Class I dye. On Chart 3.A, you find that this will take 1/16 teaspoon of dye.

In order to do this, predissolve 1/8 teaspoon of dye in one cup of water. This is twice the amount of dye you need. Use one half cup of this solution in your measuring in place of the powdered dye. Lower the amount of water you need to dissolve the dye to accomodate this half cup of water. In other words, you will be adding one half cup of dye solution to 1-1/2 cups of water. This equals a total of 2 cups of dye liquid that you add to the dyebath.

Example You want to dye one half yard of fabric a medium-light color, using PRO Blue 404. This is a Class III dye. On Chart 3.C, you find that this will take 5/32 teaspoon of dye.

In order to do this, predissolve 5/8 teaspoon of dye in one cup of water. This is 4 times the amount of dye you need. Use one quarter cup of this solution in your measuring in place of the powdered dye. Lower the amount of water you need to dissolve the dye to accomodate this quarter cup of water. In other words, you will be adding one quarter cup of dye solution to 1-3/4 cups of water. This equals a total of 2 cups of dye liquid that you add to the dyebath.

On Chart 3 there are places which I have marked with an asterisk (*) which would

need even smaller fractions of teaspoons. In these situations, you can measure out and predissolve a larger amount of dye and then use a smaller portion of it as was suggested in the examples above. Because the portions of predissolved dye will be also getting very small, I suggest you use Basic Concentrates. These are explained in the next chapter.

Only dissolve the dye you can use within a 3-5 day period. **Do not reuse dyebaths.** Once the dye is mixed with the soda ash, its shelf life is reduced to 15 minutes.

You now have nearly enough information for your first project. Now read Chapter 10 on how to dye and do Project #1: Three Dyebaths. Use the project description as a planning sheet while you are using Chapter 10 as a dyeing guide.

PROJECT #1:

3 Dyebaths

Fabric: 1/2 yd Quilt-cotton per dyepot (Total: 1-1/2 yards)

Measurement Method: Dyebath by Dyebath

Measuring Equipment: 3 dye pots, 1 two-cup measure, 1 set of measuring spoons, and 6 8-oz plastic containers. See Chapter 6 for remaining equipment.

Dyes Needed: PRO Blue 404 (Chart 3.C)
Red MX-5B (Chart 3.C)
Yellow MX-4G (Chart 3.B)

1. Deep Yellow   (4%owf)   (5/8 tsp of Yellow MX-4G)

2. Deep Blue   (4%owf)   (3/4 tsp of PRO Blue 404)

3. Medium Red   (1.5%owf)   (3/8 tsp Red MX-5B)

Preparation

Dyepots: Put in dyepots: 3 T salt
1 tsp water softener (only if needed)
2 C warm water (100º F)

Dye: Measure & dissolve dye for each dyebath in 2 cups warm water (100º F).

Alkali: Dissolve for each dyepot: 2-1/4 tsp soda ash in 1 C **hot** water (140º F).

See Chapter 10, "How to Dye," for complete information.

Calculating How Much Dye To Use

To determine how much dye to use, multiply the percentage strength of the color desired by the weight of the fabric. The resulting number is the weight of the dye you will need. Because of the small weights being measured, I use metric measurement, and then convert the weight of the dye into teaspoons.

The examples below use the standard dye weight, Class III. The calculations are worked in metric. The dye weight is then converted to teaspoons. I have rounded down the metric equivalent, 453.6 grams, of one pound to 450 grams. Similarly, one ounce has been rounded down to 28 grams. For these examples, **a teaspoon of dye weighs 3 grams**

Example You want to dye 1 pound of fabric a dark color. This takes a 4%owf amount of dye. 4% of 1 pound is 0.04 x 450 grams, or 18 grams. Dividing 18 by 3, this is 6 teaspoons. Since there are 3 teaspoons in a tablespoon, this is also 2 tablespoons of dye.

Example You want to dye 1 pound of fabric a medium color. This is a 2%owf amount of dye. 2% of one pound is 0.02 x 450 grams, or 9 grams of dye. Dividing 9 by 3, this is 3 teaspoons of dye. Since there are 3 teaspoons in a tablespoon, this is also 1 tablespoon.

Example You want to dye one half yard (2 ounces) of quilt-cotton black. This takes an 8%owf amount of dye. 8% of 2 ounces is 0.08 x 56 grams, or 4.5 grams. Dividing 4.5 by 3, this is 1-1/2 teaspoons.

CHAPTER 9.

Basic Concentrate System

The method described in Chapter 8 for measuring and dissolving dye is adequate when doing a small number of dyebaths or working with a variety of fabrics of different weights. Consider the following situations:

* Within a dye session you are planning to do more than 4 dyebaths, all of the same weight of fabric.

* You are planning to dye the same weight of fabric over a period of several days and would like to do all your dye mixing at one time.

The dye measuring can be simplified by measuring the dyes collectively and mixing them into "Basic Concentrates." In this chapter I explain the Basic Concentrate System, and how to use it for any fabric. A comprehensive chart (Chart 5) is included for using Basic Concentrates with quilt-cotton.

Using Basic Concentrates: What They Are and Why Use Them

When many fabrics of the **same** weight are dyed in a dye session, more than likely the same dyes are used over and over again in various ways: to make blended colors, light colors, dark colors, etc. If you use the method described in Chapter 8, you have to measure from the same dye jar many times. This can be avoided by measuring and dissolving each dye collectively. The liquid is then divided up into the proper dyebaths.

There are several advantages to this. (1) The amount of time spent working with the powdered dye is minimized. (2) The amount of time spent wearing a face mask (which tends to cloud up my glasses) is lessened. (3) Dye sessions are shorter because less time is spent measuring dye. (4) The small amounts of dye needed for pale colors are easier to measure because they are being measured as part of a larger amount of dye.

In order for this to work smoothly, I needed a system for dividing up the dye concentrate so each dyepot has the right amount of dye. During my dye sessions, I often dye many pieces of either 1/2 or 1/4 yard of quilt-cotton. I needed a system that would work for these small amounts of fabric and the small amounts of water in which they are dyed.

I also needed to accomodate the large amounts of fabric I occasionally dye. Because the dye is only soluble up to 6 teaspoons per cup, I needed a way to insure the dye would dissolve.

The system I have designed is called the "Basic Concentrate System." It is defined twice: once for less than one pound of fabric, and once for more than one pound solves properly. Here is its definition for less than one pound of fabric:

**Basic Concentrate for
Less than One Pound of Fabric**

A Basic Concentrate is a dye concentrate in which one cup of concentrate contains a 4%owf amount of a particular dye for a given amount of fabric (less than one pound) at a 20:1 water to fiber ratio.

Example These are Basic Concentrates. Use Chart 5 to check the dye quantities.

1 C PRO Blue 404 Basic Concentrate containing 1-1/2 tsp dye, used to dye **one yard** of quilt-cotton.

1 C Yellow MX-4G Basic Concentrate containing 5/8 tsp dye, used to dye **one half yard** of quilt-cotton.

1 C Red MX-5B Basic Concentrate containing 3/8 tsp dye, use to dye **one quarter yard** of quilt-cotton.

The amounts of dye contained in the concentrate will change depending on the quantity of fabric being dyed and the density of the dye. The value of the color for the amount of concentrate being mixed will not change.

The above definition is written for dyeing less than one pound of fiber (four yards of quilt-cotton). If you are dyeing more than one pound of fiber at a time,

you need to adjust this definition. This insures that the dye dissolves completely.

**Basic Concentrate for
One Pound or More of Fabric**

A Basic Concentrate is a dye concentrate in which two cups of concentrate contains a 4%owf amount of a particular dye for a given amount of fabric (one pound or more) at a 20:1 water to fiber ratio.

Instead of one cup, use **2 cups of water** to dissolve a 4%owf amount of dye for **one pound or more of fiber**. (See Chart 5.A: Four Yards.)

In order to avoid constant repetition and possible confusion, the remainder of this chapter will be written from the standpoint of dyeing less than one pound of fiber. **Double the amounts of concentrate to get the liquid amounts needed for dyeing one pound or more of fiber.**

When I refer in the upcoming discussion to one cup or one half cup of Basic Concentrate, I will be referring back to the definition for less than one pound of fabric. One cup of Basic Concentrate produces a deep hue (standardly a 4%owf). Two cups produce a very deep hue (8%owf). Anything less than one cup produces a medium down to a very pale hue. Most dyes show a deepening of color when dyed with 2 cups of Basic Concentrate. Some bright colors, such as yellow and turquoise, are their deepest with one cup of Basic Concentrate.

The Basic Concentrate system has additional benefits. The relationship described between cups of concentrate and strength of color can simplify color mixing discussions. A Basic Concentrate describes a relationship between an unspecified fabric and an unspecified dye. They are related by the fact that one cup of Basic Concentrate produces a deep hue of that dye on that amount of fabric. Examples can be given in a generalized form, instead of having to state the weight of fabric or the measured amount of powdered dye.

Color recipes are also simple to write using Basic Concentrates. They can be used on fabrics other than those which were originally dyed. When I write a color recipe, I list the amount of Basic Concentrate, the "%owf," as well as the amount of dye and fabric. If later I want to dye a different amount of fabric that same color, I know I will need to mix the same amount of Basic Concentrate in the strength appropriate for that fabric's weight.

How to Mix and Use Basic Concentrates

Use Basic Concentrates when you are preparing more than four dyepots, and/or using 2 or more dye colors to dye several (or more) fabrics of the same weight. Use this procedure:

Mixing Basic Concentrates

Step 1: Write down your dye plans. (Use the sample projects as guides)

Step 2: List separately the amount of Basic Concentrate(s) needed for each dyebath.

Step 3: Total up the amount of Basic Concentrate to be mixed for each dye that you are using in that dye session.

Step 4: Determine the amounts of each dye needed. Use the information from Chart 3, Charts 4 and 5, this chapter, and/or Chapter 8.

Step 5: Use one beaker or pitcher for each dye concentrate. Sprinkle the measured dye into the amount of water needed, and stir until dissolved. Repeat for each concentrate. Observe all the safety precautions mentioned in Chapter 4.

Here is an example based on Project #3:

Example

Step 1: I plan to dye a color wheel with deep values of each color. I intend to dye one-half yard pieces of quilt-cotton and to use these dyes: PRO Blue 404, Yellow MX-4G, and Red MX-5B.

Step 2: These are the amounts of Basic Concentrate I need for each dyepot:

1. 1 C PRO Blue 404
2. 1 C Red MX-5B
3. 1 C Yellow MX-4G
4. 1/2 C Yellow MX-4G and 1/2 C PRO Blue 404
5. 1/2 C Yellow MX-4G and 1/2 C Red MX-5B
6. 1/2 C PRO Blue 404 and 1/2 C Red MX-5B

Step 3: I total up the amounts of Basic Concentrate needed for dye:

PRO Blue 404:   1 C + 1/2 C + 1/2 C = 2 cups

Red MX-5B: 1 C + 1/2 C + 1/2 C = 2 cups

Yellow MX-4G: 1 C + 1/2 C + 1/2 C = 2 cups

Step 4: I determine how much dye I need for 2 cups of each Basic Concentrate. I look up the weight classes of the dyes on Chart 4, and turn to the listings for one-half yard of quilt-cotton on Chart 5.

PRO Blue 404 (Class III) : 2 C Basic Concentrate contain 1-1/2 tsp dye.

Red MX-5B (Class III) : 2 C Basic Concentrate contain 1-1/2 tsp dye.

Yellow MX-4G (Class II) : 2 C Basic Concentrate contain 1-1/4 tsp dye

Step 5: I need three beakers, one for each color. Each will contain 2 cups of Basic Concentrate.

When the dye concentrates are mixed and you are ready to add them to the dyepots, work from line to line on your planning sheet. Follow this measuring procedure:

Measuring Basic Concentrates

Step 1: Measure the concentrate(s) for the first dyebath into a two cup measure.

 (i) If the amount of liquid in the measure doesn't add up to **two cups**, add water until it does.

 (ii) If the amount of liquid in the measure adds up to **two cups,** add nothing.

The amount of liquid in the measure **must** equal two cups since this amount had been subtracted from the dyebath water for dissolving the dye.

(If you are dyeing more than one pound of fiber, substitute "4" (four) for "2" (two).)

Step 2: Stir the concentrate.

Step 3: Add it to the dyepot.

Step 4: Go on to the next line on your planning sheet and the next dyepot.

Using the Basic Concentrate Charts (Chart 5.A-D)

Chart 5 indicates how much dye is needed in various quantities of Basic Concentrate for different amounts of quilt-cotton. They can also be used on those fabrics which weigh four yards to the pound, using these equivalencies (rounded down for convenience):

Four yards weigh 1 lb, or 450 gms
One yard weighs 4 oz or 112.5 gms
One-half yard weighs 2 oz, or 56 gms
One-quarter yard weighs 1 oz, or 28 gms

Chart 4 summarizes the information on dye weight classes and dyes that appeared on Chart 3 in Chapter 8. It will help you use Chart 5.

Here's how to use the charts. First, find your dye on the dye weight class chart, Chart 4. Then go to the chart for your amount of fabric. Find the listing for the amount of concentrate you need. Remember that a deep hue is 4%owf or one cup, a medium hue is 2%owf or one half cup, and so on. (On the Four Yards Chart (Chart 5.A), 4%owf is two cups, etc.) Slide your finger to the right to find the dye class listing for your dye. This tells you how much powdered dye is contained in that amount of concentrate.

Example You need 1 cup of Red MX-5B Basic Concentrate to dye one half yard of quilt-cotton. This is a Class III dye. On the One Half Yard Chart (Chart 5.C), 1 cup of Basic Concentrate takes 3/4 teaspoon of dye for a Class III dye.

If you need a larger amount of concentrate than is listed on the chart, break the number down into numbers that are there.

Example You need a total of 3 cups of PRO Blue 404 Basic Concentrate to dye several 1/2 yard pieces of quilt-cotton. The chart doesn't list the amounts for 3 cups, but it does lists dye amounts for 2 cups and 1 cup (1 + 2 = 3). Locate the amounts of dye at each of those lines (2 cups takes 1-1/2 teaspoons, 1 cup takes 3/4 teaspoons) and add them together. For 3 cups of Pro Blue 404 concentrate, you need 2-1/4 tsp of dye.

If you need an amount of concentrate that is between two amounts listed on a chart, add the two amounts together and divide by two.

Example For 3/4 cups of Red MX-5B Basic Concentrate (see Chart 5.C) to be used on 1/2 yard of quilt-cotton, you would need 9/16 teaspoons of dye. (1/2 cup takes 3/8 teaspoon, 1 cup takes 3/4 teaspoon. 3/8 + 3/4 = 9/8. If you divide 9/8 by two, you get 9/16 teaspoon.)

As the rather frustrating example above shows, the information on Chart 5 is very complete. Occasionally, the measurements of the powdered dye and/or the concentrates will be very small. The main way to avoid this is to mix more concentrate than you need. Any amounts you don't need can be used to dye Mystery Fabric, saved up to 3-5 days, or thrown

Fabric, saved up to 3-5 days, or thrown away.

Example You want to dye one half yard of fabric with 1/4 cup of PRO Blue 404 Basic Concentrate. This would take 3/16 teaspoon of dye. Instead, mix 1/2 cup of Basic Concentrate which would take 3/8 teaspoon of dye. Use 1/4 cup of it for your fabric.

Here are two other ways to deal with the problem:

(1) Use a plastic syringe pipette for measuring liquid quantities smaller than 1/8 cup. See Chapter 21 for equivalency from cups to milliliters or cubic centimeters.

(2) By doing a Gradation Series, some situations which involve small quantities of dye or Basic Concentrate may be avoided. See Chapters 15 and 16.

Plastic Syringe Pipette

CHART 4

Dye Weight Classes

CLASS I DYES: 1 tsp weighs 4.5 gms

PRO Fuchsia 308 MX-8B

CLASS II DYES: 1 tsp weighs 3.5 gms

PRO Yellow 114 MX-4G	Cerulean Blue MX-G (Cerulean Blue)
PRO Blue 400 MX-R	B/F #2 Bright Yellow MX-4G
PRO Cobalt Blue 406 MX-G	B/F #25 Turquoise MX-G (pre-1988)

CLASS III DYES: 1 tsp weighs 3 gms

PRO Yellow 108 MX-8G	PRO Black 600 MX-CWA	B/F #28 Blue Green MX-CBA
PRO Orange 202 MX-2R	PRO Grey 601	B/F #30 Emerald Green
PRO Red 305 MX-5B	PRO Violet 810	B/F #32 Olive Drab
PRO Blue 404	B/F #14 Coral	B/F #37 Bronze
PRO Chino 500	B/F #19A Lilac	B/F #38 Khaki
PRO Brown 505 MX-5BR	B/F #21 Teal Blue	Red MX-GBA (Earth Guild)

CLASS IV DYES: 1 tsp weighs 2.5 gms

PRO Black 602	PRO Purple 804

CLASS V DYES: 1 tsp weighs 2.25 gms

PRO Olive 708	PRO Yellow MX-GR

CLASS VI DYES: 1 tsp weighs 2 gms

Midnight Blue MX-RB (C.B)	B/F #4 Deep Yellow MX-3RA
PRO Navy 420c MX-RB 150%	B/F #22 Cobalt Blue

CHART 5.A-B

Basic Concentrate Charts for Quilt-cotton

CHART 5.A: BASIC CONCENTRATE CHART FOR FOUR YARDS						
FOUR YARDS	CLASS I	CLASS II	CLASS III	CLASS IV	CLASS V	CLASS VI
4 C (8%owf)	8 tsp	10 tsp	12 tsp	14 tsp	16 tsp	18 tsp
2 C (4%owf)	4 tsp	5 tsp	6 tsp	7 tsp	8 tsp	9 tsp
1 C (2%owf)	2 tsp	2-1/2 tsp	3 tsp	3-1/2 tsp	4 tsp	4-1/2 tsp
1/2 C (1%owf)	1 tsp	1-1/4 tsp	1-1/2 tsp	1-3/4 tsp	2 tsp	2-1/4 tsp
1/4 C (0.5%owf)	1/2 tsp	5/8 tsp	3/4 tsp	7/8 tsp	1 tsp	1-1/8 tsp
1/8 C (0.25%owf)	1/4 tsp	(5/16 tsp)	3/8 tsp	(7/16 tsp)	1/2 tsp	(9/16 tsp)

CHART 5.B: Basic Concentrate Chart for One Yard						
ONE YARD	CLASS I	CLASS II	CLASS III	CLASS IV	CLASS V	CLASS VI
2 C (8%owf)	2 tsp	2-1/2 tsp	3 tsp	3-1/2 tsp	4 tsp	4-1/2 tsp
1 C (4%owf)	1 tsp	1-1/4 tsp	1-1/2 tsp	1-3/4 tsp	2 tsp	2-1/4 tsp
1/2 C (2%owf)	1/2 tsp	5/8 tsp	3/4 tsp	7/8 tsp	1 tsp	1-1/8 tsp
1/4 C (1%owf)	1/4 tsp	(5/16 tsp)	3/8 tsp	(7/16 tsp)	1/2 tsp	(9/16 tsp)
1/8 C (0.5%owf)	1/8 tsp	(5/32 tsp)	(3/16 tsp)	(7/32 tsp)	1/4 tsp	(9/32 tsp)

CHART 5.C-D

Basic Concentrate Charts for Quilt-cotton

CHART 5.C: BASIC CONCENTRATE CHART FOR ONE HALF YARD OF QUILT- COTTON						
ONE HALF YARD	CLASS I	CLASS II	CLASS III	CLASS IV	CLASS V	CLASS VI
2 C (8%owf)	1 tsp	1-1/4 tsp	1-1/2 tsp	1-3/4 tsp	2 tsp	2-1/4 tsp
1 C (4%owf)	1/2 tsp	5/8 tsp	3/4 tsp	7/8 tsp	1 tsp	1-1/8 tsp
1/2 C (2%owf)	1/4 tsp	(5/16 tsp)	3/8 tsp	(7/16 tsp)	1/2 tsp	(9/16 tsp)
1/4 C (1%owf)	1/8 tsp	(5/32 tsp)	(3/16 tsp)	(7/32 tsp)	1/4 tsp	(9/32 tsp)
1/8 C (0.5%owf)	(1/16 tsp)	*	(3/32 tsp)	*	1/8 tsp	*

CHART 5.D: BASIC CONCENTRATE CHART FOR ONE QUARTER YARD OF QUILT-COTTON						
ONE QUARTER YD	CLASS I	CLASS II	CLASS III	CLASS IV	CLASS V	CLASS VI
2 C (8%owf)	1/2 tsp	5/8 tsp	3/4 tsp	7/8 tsp	1 tsp	1-1/8 tsp
1 C (4%owf)	1/8 tsp	(5/16 tsp)	3/8 tsp	(7/16 tsp)	1/2 tsp	(9/16 tsp)
1/2 C (2%owf)	(1/16 tsp)	(5/32 tsp)	(3/16 tsp)	(7/32 tsp)	1/4 tsp	(9/32 tsp)
1/4 C (1%owf)	(1/32 tsp)	*	(3/32 tsp)	*	1/8 tsp	*
1/8 C (0.5%owf)	*	*	*	*	(1/16 tsp)	*

Calculating Basic Concentrates for Other Fabric Weights

When you are dyeing fabrics other than quilt-cotton and want to use Basic Concentrates, you will need to calculate the amounts of Basic Concentrate needed. The calculation for this may seem awesome, but I will break it down into small steps to ease the confusion. Imagine the following situation:

Number of Dyebaths: 4
Weight of Each Piece of Fabric: 6 oz
Color Strengths to be Dyed: 4%owf, 3%owf, 1%owf, 0.5%owf
Dye: PRO Blue 404

Use your calculator:

Step 1: Convert the weight of a single piece of fabric to grams. One ounce weighs 28.5 grams (rounded down for convenience).

6 x 28.5 = 171 gms fabric

Step 2: Add together the percentage strengths (%owf) of each dye you will using. In this case there is only one dye.

4%owf + 3%owf + 1%owf + 0.5%owf = 8.5%owf

Step 3: Multiply the gram weight of the single piece of fabric by the total %owf of the dye color you need. (Rewrite the %owf as a decimal.)

0.085 x 171 = 14.535 gms dye

Step 4: Divide the gram weight of the dye by the teaspoon weight of the dye for its weight class, using the list in this chapter. PRO Blue 404 is a Class III dye. One teaspoon of it weighs 3 grams.

14.535 ÷ 3 = 4.845, or approximately 4-7/8 tsp dye

You will need 4-7/8 teaspoon of PRO Blue 404.

Step 5: Determine the amounts of Basic Concentrate you need.
4%owf needs 1 C, 3%owf needs 3/4 C, 1%owf needs 1/4 C, 0.5%owf needs 1/8 C.

1 + 3/4 + 1/4 + 1/8 = 2-1/8 C Basic Concentrate

Mix 4-7/8 teaspoon of PRO Blue 404 into 2-1/8 cups of water to dye the four pieces of fabric that each weigh 6 oz.

After you have done this much math, **save your results.** If you use the same weight of fabric over and over, you may want to make a chart for it similar to those in this book.

Projects using Basic Concentrates begin following Chapter 13: Basic Color Theory. The first project (Project #3) is a color wheel. This project is identical to Project #2 which precedes it except it uses Basic Concentrates. Compare the two to see the differences in the methods.

CHAPTER 10.

How to Dye

Using all the information from the previous sections, here's how to dye the fabric. I give a dyeing procedure synopsis and time schedule below. I strongly suggest that you compare it with the description of the chemical process of dyeing found in Chapter 3. Step 1 is preparatory. Steps 2 through 5 are the adsorbtion stage. Steps 6 and 7 are the exhaust stage. Lastly, Steps 8 and 9 are the scouring stage. Following the synopsis is a detailed step by step explanation of how to dye and some dyeing tips.

Dyeing Procedures: Synopsis and Time Schedule

1. Measure water into dyepots; prepare fabric; dissolve dye and/or mix concentrates; dissolve soda for each dyepot in individual cups; premeasure water softener and salt for each dyepot into a separate cup (optional).

2. Add salt and water softener to dyepots. Dissolve.

3. Add dissolved dye. Mix liquids in dyepots thoroughly.

4. Add dampened fabric. Rearrange fabric so dye coats it completely. Try to keep fabric completely submerged.

5. Over the next 15 -20 minutes, rearrange fabric every 3 to 5 minutes.

6. Remove fabric from the dyepot, add dissolved soda ash. Mix up the liquids. Replace fabric. Rearrange fabric so the soda ash disperses throughout fabric for several minutes. Most of the chemical reaction occurs now.

7. Over the next 50 minutes, rearrange fabric every 5 to 10 minutes.

8. Empty dyepots. Rinse fabric to remove all soda ash.

9. Wash and dry fabric.

Now let's look at the dyeing procedure in some detail.

A. Decide what you are doing. Make a planning sheet. (See Chapter 12 for directions and use the projects in the book as samples.) Determine the ingredient amounts for each dyepot. Put the sheet up in your work area where you can see it.

B. Prepare fabric. The fabric should have no finishes and should have been prescoured in hot (140º F) water in a washing machine, using 1 teaspoon of soda ash and 1 teaspoon of Synthrapol for every pound of fabric you place in your washing machine.

If your fabric tends to curl at the edges when it is washed, tear off the selveges. Clip a small piece off of all four corners of the fabric to cut down on ravelling. Remove all long ravelling threads so they don't create marks on the surface of your fabric while it is being dyed. Mark the fabric if you are coding it. (See Chapter 12.)

Wet the fabric evenly and wring out any extra water. Fold the coded fabric so you can see the code numbers, and stack it up in numerical order.

C. Measure the water into the dyepots. The water should be at room temperature (75º - 95º F). Temperatures that are too low will slow down or completely stop the dyeing reaction.

Remember that the water you are adding at this time is only a portion of the total water needed for the dyebath. You will add the remaining water later with the dye and the soda ash. Use the suggestions at the bottom of Chart 1 for dividing up the water.

D. Add the salt and the water softener. Measure the amount of salt and water softener (only if needed) for each dyepot. If you have more than three dyepots, save time by premeasuring the salt and softener together into individual containers (one per dyepot). Then add to the dyepots.

At this point, you should be wearing rubber gloves, even though there is no dye in use. If your hands get wet before you put on the gloves, the gloves will be difficult to get on, and they will get wet and clammy inside.

Stir to dissolve the salt and the water softener. If you place the fabric in the dyepot before the salt is dissolved, your fabric will be blotchy. If you are dyeing one quarter yard of quilt-cotton, the salt and water softener will not dissolve at this time, as there is not enough liquid in the dyepot. They will dissolve easily after you add the dye.

E. Prepare the dyes. Fill one or two half gallon pitchers with warm water. Do not use water warmer than 100º F because it will speed up the hydrolization. If you have very hard water, add water softener to these pitchers. Refer to your planning sheet and work methodically. **Wear a face mask, safety goggles, and rubber gloves while measuring the dyes.**

Mixing Directions for Measuring Dye by the Dyebath:

For less than one pound of fabric: Sprinkle the measured dye(s) into a measuring container which contains **two** cups of warm (100º F) water. Stir to dissolve. Add this entire amount to the dyepot. Repeat for each dyepot.

For one pound or more of fabric: Sprinkle the measured dye(s) into a measuring container which contains **four** cups of warm (100º F) water. Stir to dissolve. Add this entire amount to the dyepot. Repeat for each dyepot.

Mixing Directions for Using Basic Concentrates:

Use the Basic Concentrate System described in Chapter 9.

For less than one pound of fabric: First, mix the amounts of Basic Concentrate needed for each color for the entire dye session. Then measure the desired concentrate(s) for the first dyepot into a 2 cup measure. If the amount of concentrate for this dyepot is less than 2 cups, add more warm (100º F) water to bring the total amount of liquid up to 2 cups. Add this to the first dyepot, and repeat for each subsequent dyebath.

For one pound or more of fabric: First, mix the amounts of Basic Concentrate needed for each color for the entire dye session. Then measure the desired concentrate(s) for the first dyepot into a 1 qt pitcher or 1000 ml beaker. If the amount of concentrate for this dyepot is less than 4 cups, add more warm (100º F) water to bring the total amount of liquid up to 4 cups. Add this to the first dyepot, and repeat for each subsequent dyebath.

Stir the liquids in each dyepot. Feel the bottom of the dyepot with your gloved hands to make sure the salt is dissolved. Rinse off your gloves in between each dyepot so the colors do not intermix.

F. Add the dampened fabric to the dyepots. Immerse the fabric in the water by pushing in the center first, and then pushing it down and out towards the sides of the dyepot while your hands are still under water. **Try to keep the fabric completely submerged in the water.** If the fabric is bulging up to the surface like a balloon, it probably has air trapped under it. "Burp" the fabric by flattening it with both of your hands.

You can also get the fabric to submerge better by reducing the surface tension of the water by adding Synthrapol to the dyebath. Use 1/2 teaspoon Synthrapol per gallon of water. If your dyebaths are small, premix this solution and measure it into your dyepots.

Rearrange the fabric in the dyepot so it is not bunched up or cramped. This is easier if your container is wide and shallow. Use your gloved fingers to creep the fabric under the dyebath. The fabric will softly pleat or fold behind your hands. It will be gently accordianed in the water so it resembles ribbon candy (or even brains!). Be sure all of the fabric is coated with dye. Rinse off your gloves before going to the next dyepot so the colors do not intermix.

G. Rearrange the fabric in the dyepots every 3 to 5 minutes over a 15 - 20 minute period. Vigorously rearrange the folds of the fabric to recoat every part of the fabric with dye. Walk your fingers through the fabric, creeping it toward you. Bring the fabric under the dyebath and back up again. Every fold will be "unfolded" and refolded in this process. Make sure the fabric does not stick to itself. If the fabric is not rearranged properly, your results will be splotchy.

H. Dissolve the soda ash in hot water. The total amount of water needed for the dyebath includes this water. Measure the **hot** water and the soda ash for each dyepot into an individual container. Stir until completely dissolved. If undissolved soda ash has contact with your fabric, your fabric will be blotchy. Place a container of dissolved soda ash next to each dyepot.

I. Add the dissolved soda ash to the dyepots at the end of the 15-20 minute cycle in the following manner, working from one dyepot to the next. (a) Take out the fabric with one hand, and hold it out of the way above the pot. (b) Pour the dissolved soda ash into the dyepot with the other hand. (c) Stir the liquids together with your free hand. (d) Replace the fabric. (e) Continuously rearrange the fabric over the next several minutes. At the end of these steps, go on to the next dyepot. Most of the chemical reaction takes place **now!** It is important that the soda ash is well distributed throughout the dyebath and fabric.

If your fabric is too heavy to remove, you can add the dissolved soda ash to the dyepots in 3 stages (1/4, 1/4, 1/2). Push the fabric to one side before you add it, and

52

fabric to one side before you add it, and agitate in between stages.

If you have more than three dyepots, you will have to go back and rearrange the fabric in them while you are adding the soda to the others. Do not do more than you can handle. If you are doing a lot of dyeing, consider working with a partner.

J. Rearrange the fabrics every 5 to 10 minutes over the next fifty minutes.

K. Empty each dyepot and rinse out the fabric from it individually. Rinse in room temperature water (75o - 95o F), using hot water for the final rinse. Be sure to remove all the soda ash. Drop the fabric into a washerful of hot water. Rinse out the dyepots.

L. Wash the fabrics in hot water in a washing machine with 2 tablespoons of Synthrapol. This removes the salt and the leftover dye so the fabric will not bleed. The dye will not stain the inside of your washing machine. It is not necessary to clean out the washer after the load is completed.

All of the freshly dyed and well rinsed fabrics can be washed together. Any dye that runs off the fabric is spent and should not be able to dye anything else.

N. Dry the fabric in the dryer or on the clothesline. The heat from the dryer is **not** necessary to "set" the dye. The dye was "set" in the dyebath when the soda ash was added.

Here are a few tips to make your dyeing sessions easier:

(1) Use a waterproof marker to indicate or highlight the two and four cup marks on your quart pitchers and beakers. If you are frequently dyeing large amounts of fabric, do the same to indicate measuring lines on the sides of your dyepots.

(2) If you have leftover dye concentrate, use it to dye "Mystery Fabric." Save one dyepot to be the "Mystery Bucket." Prepare this container in the same way as the other dyepots. Add all the leftover dye concentrate to this dyepot from that dye session. The Mystery Fabric will probably be some unusual but usable color. If you don't like it, overdye it on another occasion.

(3) Fill the tub of your washing machine before your dye session is over, so it is ready when you begin emptying the dyepots and rinsing the fabric. Remember to turn the washer off when it begins to agitate.

(4) Premeasure all the soda ash and hot water you need for a dye session in advance into a plastic container with a tight lid. Shake vigorously to dissolve the soda ash. Then measure the dissolved soda ash into the cups for each dyepot.

CHAPTER 11.

Troubleshooting

Despite all your care and efforts, you will produce some dyed fabrics with disappointing results. This may happen frequently at first, but your dyeing abilities will improve. Don't throw the "bad" fabrics away. They can be overdyed to produce some interesting effects. I like to add them to the Mystery Bucket for a real surprise!

Unsuccessful fabrics may have splotches, circles, dark blotches, streaks, and uneven coloration. In general, these can be caused by:

(a) hard water
(b) dyeing in a container that is too small
(c) inadequate rearranging of fabric

Other problems and some suggestions for avoiding them are listed below.

Circles If there are light colored circles like water marks on your fabric, your fabric may not have been sufficiently prescoured. Use Synthrapol instead of detergent. Prescour with 1 teaspoon soda ash and 1 teaspoon Synthrapol per pound of fabric in hot water. Fabrics with a lot of sizing may take two prescourings.

Dark blotches This problem can have several causes. (1) Some dye spilled on the fabric before the entire piece was covered with dye. (2) The dye adsorbed unevenly due to undissolved salt or soda ash. (3) The dye was not thoroughly dissolved. (4) The fabrics were not rinsed thoroughly to remove the soda ash after they were dyed and became polluted in the washing machine.

Splotches and uneven color These problems usually result from the general reasons listed at the beginning of this discussion. Here are two other potential causes:

(1) If the temperature of the liquid in the dyepots drops quickly, the dye will not "step" evenly. Do not place your dyepots on a cold surface (like a basement or garage floor in the winter). Avoid working in cold or drafty rooms. You can help maintain the temperature of your dyebaths by covering the dyepots with plastic wrap or by setting the dyepot in a larger pan that contains hot water.

(2) Your fabric may be grabbing the dye too quickly. This problem is more noticeable with light hues since the darker hues tend to cover up the unevenness. To slow down the adsorption, you can (a) lessen the amount of salt up to one-half on light values, and/or (b) add the dissolved soda ash in 3 stages (1/4, 1/4, 1/2). Some dyers find this problem is more prevalent with the fuchsia (Fuchsia MX-8B) and red dyes and with some blues.

Bleeding Normally, fabrics dyed with Procion MX dyes do not bleed because the dyes are fiber reactive. The dye chemically reacts with the fabric after the soda ash has been added. If your fabrics bleed, it is because they were not rinsed and/or washed thoroughly. Using Synthrapol should help prevent this problem.

This problem also arises when the fabric is dyed with **NO** soda ash. If you forget the soda ash, the dye will not react permanently to the fabric. By placing a container of dissolved soda ash next to each dyepot, it is easier to remember which ones got the soda ash and which ones didn't.

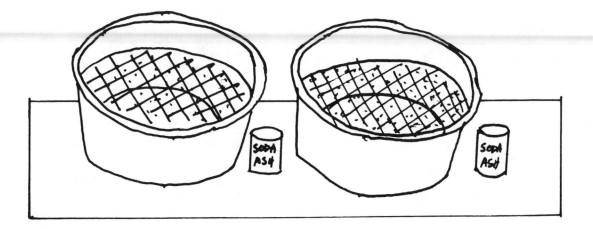

Place dissolved soda ash in individual containers next to dyepots.

CHAPTER 12.

Record Keeping

When you dye fabric, you should keep some kind of records. This helps you avoid making the same mistakes, repeat successful results, and mix new colors.

Planning Sheets

Before you begin any dye session, make a planning sheet. Decide how many dyebaths you will be doing. Indicate the amounts of all ingredients needed and the yardages (or weights) of all fabrics to be dyed in that session. On a sheet of paper, number down one side the number of dyebaths you will be doing. At each number write down color information about that particular dyebath: what color dye, and how much dye or dye concentrate will be going into that particular dyepot. If you are using the Basic Concentrate System described in Chapter 8, you can add up the listings for each color to determine the total amount of concentrate to mix of each color.

The projects in this book are written as sample planning sheets. Use them as guides.

Coding Fabrics

I like to code my fabrics so I can match my fabrics to the formulas I used on the planning sheet, and analyse my results.

Often when I dye similar colors, the coded fabric is the only way I know which formula gave me which colors. If I do a lot of dyeing over a few days, I may not get a chance to analyse my results right away. There is no guessing if you have coded your fabric.

Using a fineline waterproof pen, I mark a number in one corner of each piece of fabric to be dyed in that session. This number corresponds to the number on the planning sheet. The number on the planning sheet also corresponds with the number I assign to the dyepot's location. (I number the location rather than the dyepot as it doesn't matter what dyepot is in which spot. It's the spot that's important.) Occasionally I draw a picture of the layout for the dyepots in my dyeing area to help me coordinate everything.

When I add the fabric to the dyepots, I am **very** careful. I want the fabric marked #1 in the dyepot at the location designated as #1. I also want to add to that container the dye concentrates that are on line #1 of my planning sheet. The first time I did this it seemed very slow and awkward. I now find that I save time by not looking at two fabrics and trying to decide which is red-orange, and which is orange-red.

When I am finished and the fabric is dry, I compare my results to my planning sheet. I can usually spot any measuring mistakes easily, although sometimes a combination of colors produces an unexpected result. With the planning sheet and the coded fabric, I can identify what combination produced that beautiful gray, or that slimy greenish brown.

Recording the Results

To record my results, I cut (minimally) a one inch square of fabric, and rubber cement it in a notebook. I like to keep my dyeing records in small loose leaf notebooks that hold 3" x 5" cards. The cards are stiff and easy to flip through. They are also easy to sort and organize. The size of the notebook is convenient and portable. Loose leaf notebooks like these can be found at university bookstores.

In my notebooks I record the formula in terms of the amount of dye (in %owf) and the amounts of concentrate (if I am using the Basic Concentrate System). I indicate all quantities of fabric, soda ash, salt, water softener, and water. I also indicate if I am dyeing in a new geographic location where the water may be different. I list the name of the dye, its manufacturer's number, and the name of distributor from whom I bought the dye. I also list information about the fabric I used. I organize groups of related colors, like gradation series, on one page. A sample record follows.

CHART 6

Sample Color Recipe

1 C PRO Blue 404 concentrate (4%owf)
   (3/4 tsp dye)

Fabric: 1/2 yd Testfabrics #400M
   Mercerised Cotton Printcloth

Ingredients:
   1-1/4 qt water
   3 T salt
   2-1/4 tsp soda ash
   2 tsp Calgon water softener
     (doubled for very hard water)

Where: Arlington Heights, IL

CHAPTER 13.

Basic Color Theory

Procion MX series fiber reactive dyes are available in a wide palette of colors which can be expanded by blending the dyes together. Guidance for doing this can be provided by a color theory because it describes the relationships between colors. It also provides some terms for describing the features of a color. This discussion begins with some color terminology.

All colors have three properties: hue, value, and chroma. **Hue** is another word for color. It could be a color produced from a specific dye, or a combination of two or more dyes. For example, just as the hue of lemon yellow is different from gold, the hue of Lemon Yellow MX-4G is different than the hue of Golden Yellow MX-GR.

The **value** of a color is its amount of lightness or darkness. By using varying amounts of the same dye, we produce different values of that color. For example, using 1 cup, 1/4 cup, 1/8 cup of Red MX-5B Basic Concentrate produces three different values of red.

The **chroma** of a color is its amount of saturation, or intensity. Some colors have more chroma, or are more intense than others. For example, just as a florescent yellow is brighter than the color of a lemon, the hue of Brilliant Yellow MX-8G is more saturated or intense than Lemon Yellow MX-4G.

Hues can also be described more specifically. A **tint** is a light hue. It is produced by using less dye, or by using a diluted dye concentrate. There is no white dye. A **shade** is a darkened hue. There are shades of pastel colors as well as shades of dark colors. A shade results from adding black, grey, brown, or a complement to a particular hue. Black results from mixing very intense hues of all three primaries. It is a very dark shade. Black, brown, and gray dyes are available.

Within a color theory, certain colors are designated as **primary.** These colors cannot be produced by mixing other colors together. All other colors, however, can be produced from mixing the primaries together in varying amounts and combinations. Most common sets of primary colors include yellow, a red, and a blue.

There are numerous sets of primaries colors. When you work with dyes, it does not matter which set of primaries you use. What is important is that you use colors that will give you the color you are looking for. For this reason, you may use more than one red (or fuchsia), yellow, and blue (or cyan) as primaries.

When the equal values of two primary colors are mixed together, you have **secondary** colors. Here are some common secondaries:

Red and yellow produce red-orange
Yellow and blue produce green
Red and blue produce purple

59

If you mix pairs of adjacent primaries and secondaries, you produce the **intermediate** colors. The hue of these intermediate colors will depend on which primaries you use. If you use red and blue as primaries, red-violet and blue-violet are intermediate colors. If you use fuchsia and cyan, red and blue are intermediate colors. Red results from mixing fuchsia with a small amount of yellow. Cyan, mixed with a small amount of fuchsia, produces blue.

Complementary colors are directly opposite each other on the color wheel, such as red and green, yellow-orange and blue-violet. Mixing two complementary colors results in browns and grays. These blends are called **tertiary** colors because quantities of all three primaries are present in the hue. The color of the tertiary depends on the intensity and the value of the complementary colors.

Basic Dye Sets

I am frequently asked which dyes I use as primaries, and which dyes to buy for a "basic set." I have used these dyes as a "basic set" for the projects in this book:

> PRO Blue 404
> Lemon Yellow MX-4G
> Red MX-5B
> Black MX-CWA
> PRO Black 602.

Any of the dyes listed below can be used as primaries. Some characteristics of these dyes and others can be found in Chapter 17, "Dye Characteristics." Because there is more than one dye that could be used for each primary, I have made several suggestions. You may also want to consider purchasing the introductory or starter kits sold by some of the dye houses.

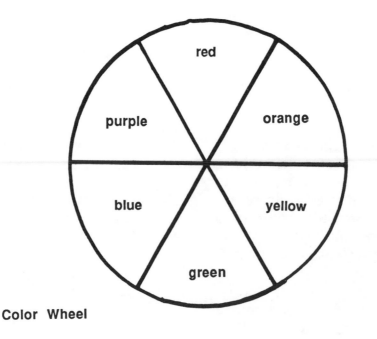

Color Wheel

60

CHART 7

Dye Recommendations

CHART 7: DYE RECOMMENDATIONS	
RED:	Fuchsia MX-8B, or Red MX-5B
YELLOW:	Brilliant Yellow MX-8G, or Lemon Yellow MX-4G
BLUE:	Turquoise MX-G, PRO Blue 404, or Cerulean Blue MX-G
BLACK:	Black MX-CWA, PRO Black 602, or B/F #44 Better Black
BROWN:	Brown MX-RDA, PRO Chino 500, or B/F #38 Khaki

Note: Check Chapter 22 for other names for these dyes. For example, Fuchsia MX-8B is sold as PRO 308 and Brooks & Flynn #13.

Note: See Chapter 17 on working with Turquiose MX-G.

PROJECT #2:

Color Wheel (Dyebath by Dyebath Method)

Fabric: 1/2 yd Quilt-cotton per dyepot
(Total: 3 yards)

Measurement Method: Dyebath by Dyebath Method

Measuring Equipment: 6 dyepots, 12 8-oz plastic containers, 1 4-cup or 1000 ml beaker, 1 two cup measure, 1 set of measuring spoons, 1 set of measuring cups. See Chapter 6 for the remaining equipment.

Dyes Needed: PRO Blue 404   (Class III)
Yellow MX-4G   (Class II)
Red MX-5B   (Class III)

1. Deep Blue   (3/4 tsp PRO Blue 404)

2. Deep Yellow   (5/8 tsp Yellow MX-4G)

3. Deep Red   (3/4 tsp Red MX-5B)

4. Medium Blue, Medium Red   (3/8 tsp PRO Blue 404
3/8 tsp Red MX-5B)

5. Medium Yellow, Medium Blue   (5/16 tsp Yellow MX-4G (See **Dye,** below)
3/8 tsp PRO Blue 404)

6. Medium Yellow, Medium Red   (5/16 tsp Yellow MX-4G (See **Dye,** below)
3/4 tsp Red MX-5B)

Preparation for Project #2

Dyepots

Put in dyepots: 3 T salt
1 tsp water softener (only if needed)
2 C warm water

Dye

In order to measure the dye, Yellow MX-4G, for Dyepots #5 & #6 with household measuring equipment, add the two amounts of dye together:

$$5/16 + 5/16 = 5/8.$$

Predissolve 5/8 tsp Yellow MX-4G dye in 1 C warm water.

Measure the other dyes directly.

Measurement

Dyepots #1-4: Measure and dissolve the powdered dye for each dyebath in 2 C warm water. Add to the dyepot.

Dyepots #5 & 6: For each dyebath, measure 1/2 C predissolved yellow dye into a 2 cup measure. Measure and add 1-1/2 C warm water to make a total of 2 C in the measure. Measure the remaining dye for the other cup into the 2 cup measure and stir to dissolve. Add to the dyepot.

Alkali

Dissolve for each dyebath: 2-1/4 tsp soda ash in 1 C **hot** water.

See Chapter 10 for information on "How to Dye."

PROJECT #3:

Color Wheel (Basic Concentrate Method)

Fabric: 1/2 yd Quilt-cotton per dyepot
(Total: 3 yards)

Measurement Method: Basic Concentrate Method

Measuring Equipment: 6 dyepots, 12 8-oz plastic containers, 3 4-cup or 1000-ml beakers, 1 two cup measure, 1 set of measuring spoons, 1 set of measuring cups. See Chapter 6 for the remaining equipment.

Dyes Needed: PRO Blue 404   (Class III)
Yellow MX-4G   (Class II)
Red MX-5B   (Class III)

1.   1 C PRO Blue 404   (4%owf)

2.   1 C Yellow MX-4G   (4%owf)

3.   1 C Red MX-5B   (4%owf)

4.   1/2 C Yellow MX-4G   (2%owf each)
     1/2 C PRO Blue 404

5.   1/2 C Yellow MX-4G   (2%owf each)
     1/2 C Red MX-5B

6.   1/2 C PRO Blue 404   (2%owf each)
      1/2 C Red MX-5B

Measure **cups of concentrate** in the above dyepots.

Preparation for Project #3

Dyepots

Put in each dyepot: 3 T salt
                                   1 tsp water softener (only if needed)
                                   2 C warm water

Concentrate

Mix:
     2 C PRO Blue 404   (1-1/2 tsp dye: 2 C water)
     2 C Yellow MX-4G   (1-1/4 tsp dye: 2 C water)
     2 C Red MX-5B   (1-1/2 tsp dye: 2 C water)

Measurement

Measure the concentrate needed for each dyepot into a 2 cup measure. Add water to bring amount of liquid up to 2 cups if necessary.

Alkali

Dissolve for each dyepot: 2-1/4 tsp soda ash in 1 C **hot** water.

See Chapter 9 and Chapter 10 for more information.

CHAPTER 14.

Color Mixing for Dyers

Here are some guidelines for mixing dyes together to produce blended hues.

(1) **The hues of some dyes do not intensify when the strength of the concentrate is raised above 4%owf.** Examples are the bright yellows (Lemon Yellow MX-4G, Brilliant Yellow MX-8G) and Turquoise MX-G. In these cases, the hue of a 4%owf strength of a dye is not much different than an 8%owf strength. If you need a more intense hue, change to a more intense dye that is similar in hue to the dye you have been using. For example, if you want a blue deeper than PRO Blue 404, switch to Cerulean Blue MX-G. You will have to experiment to determine which dyes blend together like this.

(2) **Dyes do not mix into hues that are darker or more intense than the dyes are themselves.** When you are mixing a dark color, use the dyes that are the most intense like Brilliant Yellow MX-8G or Fuchsia MX-8B, rather than medium chroma dyes like Lemon Yellow MX-4G or Red MX-5B.

(3) **When you mix dyes together for a very deep hue like deep purple, dark walnut, or deep kelly green, you may have to use 4%owf or more of one, the other, or both dyes.** Use the most intense dyes for these color blending situations, as recommended above.

The amount of concentrate needed for these recipes may exceed the amount of water you have partitioned from the total amount of water needed for the dyebath. To avoid diluting your dyebath inadvertantly, mix stronger concentrates.

(4) **When mixing a light color and a deep color, darken the light color, rather than using the light color to change the dark.** When mixing with yellow, the amount of the other hue will be quite small. For example, mix orange by adding a small amount of Red MX-5B to Yellow MX-8G, rather than adding huge amounts of Yellow to Red.

Remember that the colors you mix yourself always are less bright than the purchased dye colors. Colors dull slightly whenever they are mixed together, when the mixture contains all three primaries, and when the mixture contains a lot of dye.

CHAPTER 15.

Color Gradations

A color gradation is a set of colors that either ranges from light to dark in value, or changes gradually from one hue to another, or both. Color gradated sets of fabric are difficult to find commercially. Their importance in quilting and other fiberarts can not be underestimated.

Color gradations tell us many things about the dyes: how strong they are, how bright they are, how fast they react. We also can learn about their color properties: color range (value), upper limits in color intensity (chroma), and hue (specific color).

When you get a new dye, get acquainted with it by doing a Simple Color Gradation before you begin using the dye to mix colors. Not doing this may produce some unforeseen and unfortunate results.

How to Do a Simple Color Gradation Series

A Simple Color Gradation Series is the easiest way to discover the above mentioned characteristics of a dye. A series of dyebaths are done which contain smaller and smaller amounts of a particular dye, beginning with a 8%owf concentrate (or in the case of very bright hues, 4%owf).

I usually work a Simple Color Gradation Series in six levels, but there can be more or less. Each level in the gradation is dyed in a separate dyepot. The levels in the gradation are achieved by adding the concentrate in a sequence so each dyepot has half as much dye as the one before it. Sometimes there will be gaps in the gradation because the dye hue does not lighten evenly. If there are gaps, they can be filled in later.

Most Simple Color Gradation Series use a total of 4 cups of Basic Concentrate. It is subdivided into these amounts: 2 cups, 1 cup, 1/2 cup, 1/4 cup, 1/8 cup, and 1/16 cup. There will be a small amount of leftover dye concentrate which can be added to the Mystery Bucket. The small amounts of concentrate listed at the end of the series do **not** need to be measured directly if you follow the procedure below. (Note: Thank you to Jan Myers-Newbury from whom I learned this method of measurement.)

Simple Color Gradation Series

0. Prepare 6 dyepots.

1. Mix 4 cups of Basic Concentrate in a 1 qt or 1000 ml container. (For very bright colors like yellow or turquoise, mix 2 cups of Basic Concentrate. Add 2 cups of warm water so you have a total of four cups of liquid.)

2. Add 2 cups of concentrate to the first dyepot. This is an 8%owf solution (4%owf if you are using yellow) and produces a very deep hue. Add two cups of warm water to the beaker to replace the two cups you measured out. This brings the total amount of liquid back to 4 cups.

3. Add 2 cups of concentrate to the second dyepot. The concentrate is now half strength (a 4%owf solution) and produces a dark hue. Add two cups of replacement water to the beaker.

4. Add 2 cups of concentrate to the third dyepot. It is now one quarter strength (a 2%owf solution) and produces a medium hue. Add two cups of replacement water to the beaker.

Repeat this last step for the fourth, fifth, and sixth dyepots, or until the concentrate is nearly colorless. Complete the dyeing procedure.

There will be six dyepots of the same hue of dye, ranging in value from very deep to light.

Measure dye into 4 cups of water in a 1 qt or 1000 ml container.

4 cups of Basic Concentrate

Measure 2 cups of concentrate into a 2 cup measure.

Add this to the first dyepot.

Add two cups of warm water to the beaker to replace the two cups you measured out.

This brings the total amount of liquid back to 4 cups.

Occasionally while mixing colors, you may want to gradate one color while mixing it with another. This same measuring process can be done with smaller amounts of Basic Concentrate. For example, you can do a color gradation with one cup of Basic Concentrate. In this case, you would begin with 1 cup of Basic Concentrate, and bring the amount of liquid in the beaker up to 2 cups. You would then add one cup of Basic Concentrate to a dyepot, and add one cup of replacement water to the beaker. The other color provides the remaining water.

Adjusting Concentrates Based on Color Value

Using the dyeing instructions found in this book, you should be able to match the colors found on the dye charts from the dye houses. When you get a new dye, do a Simple Color Gradation Series before you begin using it to mix colors. Compare the darkest fabric you dyed to the swatch for that dye from the dye house where you bought the dye. This will determine whether or not you are using the dye to its fullest color potential.

Sometimes you will find that the strength of the concentrate needs to be adjusted, based on the information obtained from the gradation. If the darkest level is not dark enough and the sixth level is very pale to white, increase the amount of powdered dye to strengthen the concentrate. If there is little difference between the first two levels, use less powder to make a weaker concentrate. Keep records of everything you do.

You may want to adjust the concentrate for your own convenience. If you do not intend to use the full range of colors for any dye, slant the concentrate to fit your needs. Save swatches and full information from the initial gradation series so you will have records of how to get the other hues. Redefine the Basic Concentrate for that dye so the one cup or one-half cup level is the depth of hue that you use the most.

Project #4 follows. It is a Simple Color Gradation Series for Black MX-CWA. Project planning sheets can be found in Chapter 20 for doing Simple Color Gradations for the dyes used in the color wheel project (PRO Blue 404, Yellow MX-4G, and Red MX-5B) and the other black dye (PRO Black 602 or B/F #44 Better Black).

PROJECT #4:

Simple Color Gradation Series

Fabric: 1/2 yd Quilt-cotton per dyepot
(Total: 3 yards)

Measuring Equipment: 6 dyepots, 12 8-oz plastic containers, one beaker, a two cup measure, and one set of measuring spoons. See Chapter 6 for the remaining equipment.

Dye Needed: Black MX-CWA   (Class III)

1. 2 C Black MX-CWA   (8%owf)

2. 1 C Black   (4%owf)

3. 1/2 C Black   (2%owf)

4. 1/4 C Black   (1%owf)

5. 1/8 C Black   (0.5%owf)

6. 1/16 C Black   (0.25%owf)

Measure **cups of concentrate** into the above dyepots.

Preparation for Project #4

Dyepots

Put in each dyepot: 3 T salt
                                    1 tsp water softener (only if needed)
                                    2 C warm water

Concentrate

Mix : 1 T Black MX-CWA in 4 C warm water

Measurement

This is a Simple Color Gradation Series.

1. Add 2 cups of concentrate to Dyepot #1. This is an 8%owf solution.

2. Add two cups of warm water to the beaker to replace the two cups you measured out. This brings the total amount of liquid back to 4 cups.

3. Add 2 cups of concentrate to Dyepot #2. The concentrate is now half strength (a 4%owf solution). Add two cups of replacement water to the beaker.

4. Add 2 cups of concentrate to Dyepot #3. It is now one quarter strength (a 2%owf solution). Add two cups of replacement water to the beaker.

Repeat this last step for Dyepots #4, #5, and #6.

Alkali

Dissolve for each dyepot: 2-1/4 tsp soda ash in 1 C **hot** water.

See Chapter 9 and Chapter 10 for more information.
See Projects #9-12 for more Simple Gradation Series.

CHAPTER 16.

Using Color Gradations

The Simple Color Gradation Series explained in Chapter 15 provides a value range for a single dye. There also are gradations that use two or more dye combinations. Four are given in this chapter. You can further combine these gradations to produce a wide variety of multi-colored effects by using the end point of one as the starting point of another. A color that results from any of these gradations can be separated from the series, mixed independently, and used to blend new colors.

Color gradations provide an endless variety of colors that can be mixed. Here are some suggestions to get you started:

(1) Mixing combinations of primary and/or secondary colors produces a wide range of **intermediate hues.**

Red MX-5B & PRO Blue 404:
    Fuchsia to lavender to blue

Yellow MX-4G & PRO Blue 404:
    Yellow to green to blue

Red MX-5B & Yellow MX-4G:
    Yellow to orange-red to fuchsia

(2) Mixing a color with its complement, brown, or gray gives different **shades**.

Red MX-5B & B/F #30 Emerald Green:
    Fuschia to soft red brown to soft green

Yellow MX-8G & B/F #19A Lilac:
    Yellow to brown to lilac

Orange MX-2R & Cerulean Blue MX-G:
    Orange to dark gray to deep blue

See Chapter 13 and Chapter 17 for more information on specific dyes.

The following gradations have been written from the standpoint that less than one pound of fabric is being dyed and 2 cups of water have been partitioned off from the total amount of water for the dyebath. If you are dyeing more than one pound of fabric and partitioning 4 cups of water from the dyebath, **double** all quantities of dye concentrate listed throughout the remainder of this chapter.

The gradations which follow can be worked with three colors as well as two. The third color can be mixed with one or the other color for the whole series, or with one color for the first part of the series, and the other color for the remainder. These suggested gradations can be extended in length, if so desired, or shortened. What matters is that you get the effect **you** want.

73

Simple Two Color Gradation

Description: Two colors are mixed together for a blended color gradation that will change in value from light to dark hues.

Method: The colors are mixed together and measured as for a Simple Color Gradation Series.

Color Suggestions: Begin by mixing pairs of primary colors together to make secondary colors. Mix each of your primaries with the different browns, grays, or blacks to see the shading possibilities. For example, combining the three primaries with the two different blacks would give you six possibilities:

> Fuchsia and Black MX-CWA
> Fuchsia and Cotton Black
> Yellow and Black MX-CWA
> Yellow and Cotton Black
> Cyan Blue and Black MX-CWA
> Cyan Blue and Cotton Black

The following project mixes Black MX-CWA with Red MX-5B. Other Simple Two Color Gradations can be found in Chapter 20. They mix each primary with each of the two blacks. Because of the differences in the formulation of each black dye, there will be differences in the colors of the mixed dyes.

Concentrate: (for 6 dyepots) 2 cups of concentrate for each color

SIMPLE TWO COLOR GRADATION SERIES						
Concentrate	Dyepot 1	Dyepot 2	Dyepot 3	Dyepot 4	Dyepot 5	Dyepot 6
Color A	1 C	1/2 C	1/4 C	1/8 C	1/16 C	1/32 C
Color B	1 C	1/2 C	1/4 C	1/8 C	1/16 C	1/32 C
Combined Measurement	2 C	1 C	1/2 C	1/4 C	1/8 C	1/16 C

Measuring Instructions for Simple Two Color Gradation

1. Mix 2 cups of Basic Concentrate for each color you will be mixing. Combine in a 1 quart or 1000 ml beaker. You will have a total of 4 cups of Basic Concentrate.

2. Add 2 cups of concentrate to the first dyepot. Add two cups of warm water to the beaker to replace the two cups you measured out. This brings the total amount of liquid back to 4 cups.

3. Add 2 cups of concentrate to the second dyepot. The concentrate is now half strength. Add two cups of replacement water to the beaker.

4. Add 2 cups of concentrate to the third dyepot. It is now one quarter strength. Add two cups of replacement water to the beaker.

Repeat this last step for the fourth, fifth, and sixth dyepots.

Project #5 combines Black MX-CWA with Red MX-5B. It will produce a set of maroon fabrics ranging in value from dark to light.

PROJECT #5:

Simple Two Color Gradation Series

Fabric: 1/2 yd Quilt-cotton per dyepot   (Total: 3 yards)

Measuring Equipment: 6 dyepots, 12 8-oz plastic containers, 1 one-qt pitcher or 1000 ml beaker, a two cup measure, and one set of measuring spoons. See Chapter 6 for the remaining equipment.

Dyes Needed: Black MX-CWA   (Class III)
                   Red MX-5B   (Class III)

1. 1 C Black MX-CWA	1 C Red MX-5B	(8%owf, combined)
2. 1/2 C Black	1/2 C Red	(4%owf, combined)
3. 1/4 C Black	1/4 C Red	(2%owf, combined)
4. 1/8 C Black	1/8 C Red	(1%owf, combined)
5. 1/16 C Black	1/16 C Red	(0.5%owf, combined)
6. 1/32 C Black	1/32 C Red	(0.25%owf, combined)

Measure **cups of concentrate** into the above dyepots.

Preparation for Project #5

Dyepots

Put in each dyepot: 3 T salt
1 tsp water softener (only if needed)
2 C warm water

Concentrate

Mix: 2 C Black MX-CWA (1-1/2 tsp dye: 2 C water)
2 C Red MX-5B (1-1/2 tsp dye: 2 C water)

Mix concentrates together in one 1000 ml beaker or 1 qt pitcher.

Measurement

This is a Simple Two Color Gradation Series.

1. Add 2 cups of concentrate to Dyepot #1. Add two cups of warm water to the beaker to replace the two cups you measured out. This brings the total amount of liquid back to 4 cups.

2. Add 2 cups of concentrate to Dyepot #2. The concentrate is now half strength. Add two cups of replacement water to the beaker.

3. Add 2 cups of concentrate to Dyepot #3. It is now one quarter strength. Add two cups of replacement water to the beaker.

Repeat this last step for Dyepots #4, #5, and #6.

Alkali

Dissolve for each dyepot: 2-1/4 tsp soda ash in 1 C **hot** water.

See Chapter 9 and Chapter 10 for more information.

See Projects #13 - 17 for more Simple Two Color Gradations.

Color Gradation with a Constant

Description: At the beginning of this gradation, the first color predominates. By the end of the gradation, it is dominated by the second, or constant color.

Method: One color is gradated and the other is measured as a constant quantity. The gradated color will lighten as it is diluted. The other retains the same intensity.

Color Suggestions: These are particularly attractive when done in a primary, secondary, or intermediate hue combined with either a complementary color or a brown tone. For example:

> PRO Blue 404 and PRO Chino 500
> Blue Green MX-CBA and B/F #38 Khaki
> Gold Yellow MX-GR and Cerulean Blue MX-G

Concentrate: (for 6 dyepots)
    2 cups of concentrate of the gradated color (Color A)
    2-1/2 cups of the constant color (Color B)

COLOR GRADATION WITH A CONSTANT						
Concentrate	Dyepot 1	Dyepot 2	Dyepot 3	Dyepot 4	Dyepot 5	Dyepot 6
Color A	1 C	1/2 C	1/4 C	1/8 C	1/16 C	0
Color B	1/2 C	1/2 C	1/2 C	1/2 C	1/2 C	1/2 C

```
┌─────────────────────────────────────────────────────────────────┐
│                                                                   │
│      Measurement for Color Gradation with a Constant              │
│                                                                   │
```

1. Into a 2 cup measuring cup:

    a. Add **one** cup of Color A dye concentrate

    b. Measure the Color B dye concentrate, and add it.

    c. Add water to bring the total amount of liquid up to 2 cups.
        Add to the dyepot.

2. Add one cup of replacement water to the concentrate beaker containing Color A.

3. Repeat Steps 1 & 2 for the entire gradation

```
└─────────────────────────────────────────────────────────────────┘
```

In this chart and the project that follows, the amount of the constant was set at 1/2 cup. It can, however, be any amount.

Project #6 combines Yellow MX-4G with PRO Blue 404. It will produce a set of fabrics changing in hue from green to blue-green.

PROJECT #6:

Color Gradation with a Constant

Fabric: 1/2 yd Quilt-cotton per dyepot   (Total: 3 yards)

Measuring Equipment: 6 dyepots, 12 8-oz plastic containers, one beaker, a two cup measure, and one set of measuring spoons. See Chapter 6 for the remaining equipment.

Dyes Needed: PRO Blue 404   (Class III)
Yellow MX-4G   (Class II)

1. 1 C Yellow MX-4G   1/2 C PRO Blue 404

2. 1/2 C Yellow MX-4G   1/2 C PRO Blue 404

3. 1/4 C Yellow MX-4G   1/2 C PRO Blue 404

4. 1/8 C Yellow MX-4G   1/2 C PRO Blue 404

5. 1/16 C Yellow MX-4G   1/2 C PRO Blue 404

6. 1/32 C Yellow MX-4G   1/2 C PRO Blue 404

Measure **cups of concentrate** into the above dyepots.

Preparation for Project #6

Dyepots
Put in dyepots: 3 T salt
1 tsp water softener (only if needed)
2 C warm water

Concentrate
Mix: 3 C PRO Blue 404   (2-1/4 tsp dye: 3 C warm water)
2 C Yellow MX-4G   (1-1/4 tsp dye: 2 C warm water)

Measurement
This is a Color Gradation with a Constant.
1. Measure into a 2 cup measuring cup:

     1 C Yellow MX-4G dye concentrate
     1/2 C PRO Blue 404 dye concentrate

Add water to bring the total amount of liquid up to 2 cups. Add to Dyepot #1.

2. Add one cup of replacement water to the yellow concentrate beaker.

3. Repeat Steps 1 & 2 for each dyepot.

Alkali
Dissolve for each dyepot: 2-1/4 tsp soda ash in 1 C **hot** water.

See Chapter 10 for information on how to dye.
See Project #18 for another Gradation with a Constant.

Same Quantity Gradation

Description There is an unblended full strength color at each end of this gradation. The two colors blend in between. The hues are slightly duller, but of the same value throughout the gradation.

Method The concentrate is directly measured with measuring cups.

Color Suggestions These gradations are very attractive when done in primaries, secondaries, or intermediate colors. A few examples are given below. In each description, the middle term of the description describes the middle of the gradation.

Fuchsia MX-8B & Cerulean Blue MX-G: Fuchsia to purple to blue
Yellow MX-8G & Turquoise MX-G: Yellow to bright green to turquoise
Deep Yellow MX-3RA & B/F #19A Lilac:
Orange yellow to dark brown to deep purple

Concentrate: (for 5 dyepots) 2-1/2 cups of each color of concentrate.

SAME QUANTITY GRADATION					
Concentrate	Dyepot 1	Dyepot 2	Dyepot 3	Dyepot 4	Dyepot 5
Color A	1 C	3/4 C	1/2 C	1/4 C	0
Color B	0	1/4 C	1/2 C	3/4 C	1 C

Measuring Instructions for Same Quantity Gradation

1. Measure each color into the beaker. There should be a total of one cup of liquid.

2. Add one cup of water to bring the total amount of liquid to be added to the dyebath up to 2 cups.

This gradation can be easily worked with more levels, i.e 7/8 & 1/8, 5/8 & 3/8, etc.

The next project is for a Same Quantity Gradation, using Yellow MX-4G and Red MX-5B. The gradation will move from yellow to orange to red-orange to red.

(Note: I first became acquainted with this method of measurement in Jan Myers-Newbury's workshop in 1984.)

PROJECT #7:

Same Quantity Gradation

Fabric: 1/2 yd Quilt-cotton per dyepot   (Total: 2-1/2 yards)

Measuring Equipment: 5 dyepots, 10 8-oz plastic containers, two 1-qt pitchers or 1000 ml beakers, a two cup measure, and one set of measuring spoons. See Chapter 6 for the remaining equipment.

Dyes Needed: Red MX-5B   (Class III)
                      Yellow MX-4G   (Class II)

1. 1 C Yellow MX-4G   ----------------

2. 3/4 C Yellow MX-4G   1/4 C Red MX-5B

3. 1/2 C Yellow MX-4G   1/2 C Red MX-5B

4. 1/4 C Yellow MX-4G   3/4 C Red MX-5B

5. ------------------   1 C Red MX-5B

Measure **cups of concentrate** into the above dyepots.

Preparation for Project #7

Dyepots
Put in dyepots: 3 T salt
1 tsp water softener (only if needed)
2 C warm water

Concentrate
Mix: 2-1/2 C Red MX-5B   (1-7/8 tsp dye: 2-1/2 C warm water)
            3 C Yellow MX-4G   (1-7/8 tsp dye: 3 C warm water)

Note: Although you only need 2-1/2 C Yellow MX-4G Basic Concentrate, this would take 1-1/4 + 5/16, or 1-9/16 tsp dye. Since this can't be measured with standard household measuring equipment, mix 3 C Yellow MX-4G Basic Concentrate instead. There will be 1/2 cup of leftover yellow concentrate.

Measurement
This is a Same Quantity Gradation.
1. Measure into a 2 cup measuring cup:

       1 C Yellow MX-4G dye concentrate

Add water to bring the total amount of liquid up to 2 cups. Add to Dyepot #1.

2. Measure into a 2 cup measuring cup:

       3/4 C Yellow MX-4G dye concentrate
       1/4 C Red MX-5B dye concentrate

Add water to bring the total amount of liquid up to 2 cups. Add to Dyepot #2.

Continue measuring the dye concentrate for Dyepots #3, #4, and #5. There will be 1/2 C Yellow MX-4G concentrate leftover.

Alkali
Dissolve for each dyepot: 2-1/4 tsp soda ash in 1 C **hot** water.

See Chapter 10 for information on how to dye.
See Project #19 for another Same Quantity Gradation.

One Up, One Down Gradation

Description: This gradation has a full strength unblended color at each end. As the colors blend and approach each other, the values become lighter.

This is a variation of the Same Quantity Gradation. It differs in that the amount of Basic Concentrate will vary in each dyepot and there will be a change in value as well as hue.

Method: A Simple Color Gradation will be done from the first to the second from the last dyepot. A second Single Color Gradation is done in a different color from the last dyepot to the second from the first dyepot.

Color Suggestions: These gradations are very attractive when done in primaries, secondaries, or intermediate colors. A few examples are given below. In each description, the middle term of the description describes the middle of the gradation.

> Blue Green MX-CBA & Orange MX-2R: Blue green to rust brown to orange
> Deep Yellow MX-3RA & Cerulean Blue MX-G:
>   Orange yellow to mossy green to deep blue
> Golden Yellow MX-GR & B/F #19A Lilac: Yellow to orange brown to lilac

Concentrate (for 6 dyepots): 2 cups of Basic Concentrate for each color.

ONE UP, ONE DOWN GRADATION						
Concentrate	Dyepot 1	Dyepot 2	Dyepot 3	Dyepot 4	Dyepot 5	Dyepot 6
Color A	1 C	1/2 C	1/4 C	1/8 C	1/16 C	0
Color B	0	1/16 C	1/8 C	1/4 C	1/2 C	1 C

Measurement for One Up, One Down Gradation

1. Beginning at one end of your row of dyepots, place one cup of Color A concentrate in Dyepot #1.

2. Continue the gradation as was done in the Simple Color Gradation Series, using **one** cup of replacement water and measuring out one cup of concentrate, for the next 4 dyepots. The last dyepot (Dyepot #6) will have no dye concentrate in it.

3. Beginning with Dyepot #6, do a second Simple Color Gradation with the second color as in Steps 1 & 2. Once again use **one** cup of replacement water and measure out one cup of concentrate, until you get to Dyepot #2.

4. Add one cup of water to Dyepots #1 and #6 which had only one cup of concentrate added to each of them. The other dyepots should have 2 cups of dye concentrate liquid in them already.

If you would like to smooth this gradation out, add more steps or levels. In-between levels for the whole series can be achieved by mixing 1-1/2 cups of concentrate for each color, adding 1/2 cup of water to bring the total liquid up to 2 cups, and repeating the whole process above.

You also could measure out some in-between levels individually. Remember to bring up the liquid amount to one cup for each color. Use a syringe pipette for directly measuring the very small quantities.

The next project is a One Up, One Down Gradation. It uses PRO Blue 404 and Red MX-5B. The gradation will range in hue and value from deep red to medium purple to deep blue.

PROJECT #8:

One Up, One Down Gradation

Fabric: 1/2 yd Quilt-cotton per dyepot (Total: 3 yards)

Measuring Equipment: 6 dyepots, 12 8-oz plastic containers, 2 one-qt pitchers or 1000 ml beakers, 1 two cup measure, 1 set of measuring spoons, 1 set of measuring cups. See Chapter 6 for the remaining equipment.

Dyes Needed: | PRO Blue 404 | (Class III)
| Red MX-5B | (Class III)

1. 1 C Red MX-5B   ------------------

2. 1/2 C Red MX-5B   1/16 C PRO Blue 404

3. 1/4 C Red MX-5B   1/8 C PRO Blue 404

4. 1/8 C Red MX-5B   1/4 C PRO Blue 404

5. 1/16 C Red MX-5B   1/2 C PRO Blue 404

6. ---------------   1 C PRO Blue 404

Measure **cups of concentrate** into the dyepots above.

Preparation for Project #8

Dyepots
Put in dyepots:　　　　　3 T salt
　　　　　　　　　　　　　1 tsp water softener (only if needed)
　　　　　　　　　　　　　2 C warm water

Concentrate
Mix:　　　　　　　2 C Red MX-5B　　　(1-1/2 tsp dye: 2 C warm water)
　　　　　　　　　2 C PRO Blue 404　　(1-1/2 tsp dye: 2 C warm water)

Measurement
This is a One Up, One Down Gradation.

1. Beginning at one end of the row of dyepots, add one cup of Red MX-5B concentrate to Dyepot #1.

2. Continue the gradation as was done in the Simple Color Gradation Series, using **one** cup of replacement water and measuring out **one** cup of concentrate, for the next 4 dyepots. Add no dye concentrate to Dyepot #6.

3. Beginning with Dyepot #6, do a second Simple Color Gradation with PRO Blue 404 as in Steps 1 & 2. Once again use **one** cup of replacement water and measure out one cup of concentrate. Do not add any PRO Blue 404 concentrate to Dyepot #1.

4. Add one cup of water to Dyepots #1 and #6 which had only one cup of concentrate added to each of them. The other dyepots should have 2 cups of dye concentrate liquid in them already.

Alkali
Dissolve for each dyepot: 2-1/4 tsp soda ash in 1 C **hot** water.

See Chapter 10 for information on how to dye.
See Project #20 for another One Up, One Down Gradation.

CHAPTER 17.

Dye Characteristics

There are many differences among the various Procion MX series fiber reactive dyes besides the obvious differences in hue. Some dyes have a denser composition than others. (See Chapter 8.) There are differences in the amount of chroma, or color intensity in similar dye colors. One dye in particular has a slightly different molecular structure. Although this list is by no means comprehensive, I have listed some characteristics of the more common dye colors.

Yellows Most yellow dyes use more dye powder to achieve a medium hue than other colored dyes. This is due to the nature of the color, not the dye. Brilliant Yellow MX-8G is the brightest and clearest yellow. Deep Yellow MX-3RA and Golden Yellow MX-GR are deep yellows that have a medium yellow hue in their lesser strengths. Golden Yellow MX-GR will change in hue when it is used in its fuller strengths. Its deeper hues are orangish like American cheese or goldenrod.

Turquoise Turquoise MX-G, and any preblended dye containing turquoise, such as Brooks & Flynn's #30 Emerald Green, requires some special considerations. The molecule of the turquoise dye is larger than that of the other dyes. Consequently, the dye has a slower reaction time. If it is left at room temperature to react, the dye would need 48 hours to come to its fullest hue.

Here are two ways to compensate for this behavior. (1) Double the amount of dye you would normally use. (2) Heat the dyebath to 140º F during the last half hour of the dyeing time to speed up the chemical reaction.

Remember that Turquoise MX-G is not a very dark color. Many blended colors that use blue in their recipes can be mixed without using turquoise. For those colors, use PRO Blue 404 or medium values of Cerulean Blue MX-G.

Fuchsia Fuchsia MX-8B (i.e. PRO 308, Brooks & Flynn #13, Fabdec's Cool Red) is frequently used as a primary in dyeing fabrics. It is a concentrated dye with a very dense composition. A small jar of it lasts a very long time. Be sure to dissolve the dye thoroughly, and stir after every addition of water. If you find this dye difficult to use, try Red MX-5B (i.e. PRO 305, Brooks & Flynn #12).

Fuchsia MX-8B, as well as the other reds, tends to grab the fabric quickly because it is salt sensitive. This may result in uneven colors. If this occurs when using these dyes, reduce the amount of salt you would normally use by 25%.

Blacks There are two black dyes. Black MX-CWA is sold by all dye houses. PRO Chemical & Dye Inc. (PRO Cotton Black 602) and Brooks & Flynn (#44 Better Black) also carry a second black dye which will produce a "blacker" black on cotton.

Black MX-CWA is only standardized as a black. It is made with a reddish base. Using lesser amounts of this dye produces mauvish grays. The Cotton Black is standardized as both a gray and a black. The Cotton Black dye has a blue base. It dilutes into bluish gray hues.

Mixing other dyes with black dye produces darker shades. They may not, however, be the shades you would expect. For example, if you mix fuchsia dye with Black MX-CWA, you get maroon. If you mix it with the other black, you get a very grapy hue. Experiment by mixing each black dye with each primary (six combinations) to see the color possibilities. In some cases you may be surprised at the results. If using black dye with other colors doesn't produce the darkened shade you want, try using a gray or a brown dye that is not slanted toward any one primary, such as Brooks & Flynn's #38 Khaki or PRO Chino 500.

Often it is difficult to dye a fabric an intensely saturated black. Sometimes the fabric needs to be dyed twice. Even then, the fabric may still not be a rich deep black. When the dye sites on the fiber molecule (where the dye chemically reacts) are used up, the fabric will no longer accept dye. In trying to dye a "black-black," be prepared to use more dye (8%-10%owf). It may also take two washings in the washing machine to remove all the excess dye from the fabric.

Non-primary Colors These dyes are useful for several reasons. (1) They can make your color blending easier. (2) They will simplify your dye recipes. (3) They will be brighter than similar hues you mix yourself. I use these non-primary colors regularly:

> Blue Green MX-CBA
> B/F #14 Coral
> Red MX-GBA
> B/F #19A Lilac
> Orange MX-2R
> B/F #21 Teal Blue
> Golden Yellow MX-GR
> B/F #22 Cobalt
> Red Brown MX-5BR
> PRO Navy 420c

Non-primary colors produce a variety of color effects when they are blended together, or when they are mixed with other colors. Try mixing complementary colors, taking the intensity and value range of the dyes into consideration.

Some interesting combinations are:

PRO Blue 404 and Gold Yellow MX-GR
Red MX-8B and B/F #30 Emerald
Cerulean Blue MX-G and Orange MX-2R
B/F #19A Lilac and Orange MX-2R

These pairings (as well as many others) result in attractive shades of grays and browns.

CHAPTER 18.

Frequently Asked Questions

Are Procion MX series fiber reactive dyes colorfast? lightfast?

When a natural fiber fabric is dyed with Procion MX dyes, the dye chemically reacts with the fabric. The fabric is both colorfast and reasonably lightfast.

Are Procion MX dyes safe to use?

The dyes are safe to use, providing the safety precautions discussed in Chapter 4 are observed.

What colors of Procion MX dyes do I buy?

If you are using the sample projects in this book, you will need: Lemon Yellow MX-4G, PRO Blue 404, Red MX-5B, Black MX-CWA, and PRO Black 602. Other names for these dyes may be found on the Dye Color Comparison Chart in Chapter 22. Other suggested dyes may be found in Chapter 13.

Procion MX series fiber reactive dyes are sold by many dye houses, some of which are listed in Chapter 23. Many of these companies carry sample kits.

How much dye do I use to get a medium color?

The answer to this question is complex, but this book should provide some guidelines for answering it. See Chapters 8 and 9, plus Charts 3 and 5.

How many dyebaths should I do at one time?

Only do as many as you can do well. Begin with one or two, then try six. From there it is up to you! Your dyeing area will also determine how many you can do. Keep your dyepots grouped together--that lone dyepot on top of the humidifier may be forgotten.

Can I reuse the dyebath?

NO! The dye that is left in the dyebath at the end of a dye session has reacted with the water and is exhausted. If you try to use it a second time, the fabric may change color, but there will be no chemical reaction. The color will wash out the first time you wash the fabric.

How long can the dyes be stored?

The powdered dyes can be stored up to 2 years if they are kept in a cool dry place. After that they slowly hydrolyze and become less reactive. To be on the safe side, only buy what you can use up in one year.

What amounts of fabric should I dye while I am first learning?

Begin with either one quarter or one half yard of quilting weight cotton.

What are the differences between Chart 3 and Chart 5?

Chart 3 organizes dyes by their weight class. Each section of the chart lists the dyes for that weight class and then states the amounts of dye needed for dyeing different color strengths (%owf) and amounts of quilt cotton.

Chart 5 is organized by the amount of quilt-cotton to be dyed. For each amount of quilt-cotton, there are listings for different amounts of Basic Concentrate and the different dye weight classes. Chart 4 summarises the list of dye weight classes and the dyes mentioned in this book.

Do I have to measure directly the tiny amounts of powdered dye and Basic Concentrate that appear in the Gradation Series and on Charts 3 and 5?

Not necessarily. Here are some ways to avoid directly measuring small quantities:

(1) Mix more concentrate than you need if an amount of dry dye or dye concentrate is smaller than you can measure directly. If you still cannot measure the amount directly, use the measurement method used in a Gradation Series. Measure out half, and replace the liquid with the same amount of water to dilute the concentrate to half strength. Repeat until you have the strength of concentrate you need.

(2) Organize your dyeing so you are doing related dyebaths in the same dye session. Use Basic Concentrates, so dry dye measurement is done collectively.

(3) Avoid them completely in a Gradation Series by using the measuring instructions found in Chapter 15.

Can I dye different fibers in the same dyepot?

Yes. You may notice that not all the fabrics dyed the same strength or value of color. This is because some fabrics dye faster than others. You will probably find that those lighter fabrics will dye at least as dark as the other fabrics when they dyed by themselves.

How can I lessen the chance that my fabric will not streak? I want to dye some very expensive fabric (or my favorite worn out cotton blouse, etc.)

Follow all the directions given in this book explicitly. Frequently rearrange your fabric in the dyepot. Give your dyeing your full attention.

For extra care, double the amount of all ingredients for your dyebath. Not all the dye will exhaust itself with the fabric (some of it will be used to dye the water), but your fabric will have more room to spread out.

Can I use Procion MX series fiber reactive dyes to overdye either commercial fabrics (printed or solid), or fabrics that I have dyed previously?

Yes. Dye them as you would any other fabric. Because most commercial cottons are permanent press, the dye will work less effectively. It may take twice the normal amount of dye to get the hue you normally would get. This is a great way to create new fabrics, revive old cotton clothing (like turtlenecks and blue jeans), etc. I like to overdye an assortment of different commercial fabrics in the same dyepot.

Most hand-dyed fabrics can be overdyed, depending on how heavily dyed they were before. There is a limit to how much dye the fabric molecules will accept.

Can I use Procion MX dyes for dyeing yarn?

Yes, providing they are made from a fiber which accepts Procion MX dyes. Yarns, especially cotton and linen ones, tend to absorb more liquid than do fabric. When you dye yarn, increase the water weight to fiber weight ratio to 30 to 1.

Can Procion MX dyes be used for tie dyeing?

Yes. Procion MX dyes will produce brilliantly colored tie dyed fabrics. Because of the strength and effectiveness of the dyes, be sure to tie your fabric very firmly. This is easier if your fabric is wet.

There are two methods for tie dyeing with Procion MX dyes. One uses the long bath dyeing method which has been covered in this book. The fabric may be tied, wadded into balls, wrapped around an object, etc. and then dyed as usual. (You can also get mottled effects by not rearranging the fabric in the dyebath, but you probably have discovered this on your own!)

The other method, called the short bath method, allows you to work with several colors at once. Pretreat your fabric by soaking it in a solution of water and soda ash (9 tablespoons soda ash to 1 gallon water). Wring out any excess solution. Mix the dye into dye paint by dissolving one tsp of dye to one cup of chemical water (9 tablespoons Urea to 1 quart water). The dye is directly applied to the folded or tied fabric with squeeze bottles, brushes, etc. Be careful not to overapply the dye. Untie the fabric. Wrap it up completely in plastic to prevent it from drying. The fabric needs to rest for 6 - 24 hours while the dye reacts with the fabric. Then unwrap, rinse, and wash thoroughly. See the general instructions on painting and tie dyeing with Procion MX dyes in the instruction sheets available from the dye houses for more information on this second method.

Can I use bleach to make a fabric lighter?

Yes. This is called discharge dyeing. The fabric color is lightened by being discharged or released by the bleach. Fabrics dyed with Procion MX series fiber reactive dyes may change in hue as well as value when discharged.

Fabrics can be discharged in a sequence in the washer. Add 4-8 cups of bleach to a washer filled with water. Begin the wash cycle and drop in a quarter yard of quilting weight fabric. Continue adding fabric every 90 seconds. An average washer will successfully discharge 6 quarter yard pieces in one washer load. Finish the washer cycle. Now wash the fabric to remove as much of the discharged dye as possible. Neutralize the fabric, and wash it again.

All bleached fabrics must be neutralized. If you do not follow this step, any bleach left in your fabric will continue to discharge. Unneutralized fabric may **disintegrate!** To neutralize, dissolve 1

tablespoon of sodium bisulfite in one quart of water. (This mixture has a strong odor. Work in a ventilated area.) Add the fabric. Let it soak for 10 minutes, then rinse and wash it. Sodium Bisulfite (also sold as "Anti-Chlor") is sold by some dyehouses. Because I do not know how the fabric will be affected by the bleach and neutralizing over a long time period, I do not guarantee any results from working with these chemicals.

CHAPTER 19.

Washing Machine Dyeing

The washing machine is great for dyeing large amounts of fabric such cotton bedspreads, heavyweight cotton sweaters, quilt backings, etc. It is also useful for dyeing small articles when you want to insure that the dyeing is even.

Most washing machines operate only when the tub containing the water, clothes, etc. weighs a certain amount. When you dye in a washer, the amounts of all the ingredients you need is based on the amount of **water** needed to operate the machine, rather than the amount of fabric to be dyed. The amount of water is then used to determine the **maximum** amount of fabric that can be dyed at that load level. If you are dyeing a smaller amount of fabric, you will still need to treat the dyebath as if the maximum amount of fabric is being dyed.

Begin by determining how much water is contained in the various load levels of your washing machine. This information can be easily obtained by calling the manufacturer or by looking in the instruction book that came with your machine.

If you cannot get the information on the amount of water for each level of your washing machine, you will have to measure it manually. Fill the washer with water, and then reset the dial to pump the water out. Place a bucket or some other measuring device under the washer hose,

and start pumping out the water. When the bucket is full, shut off the washer, empty the bucket, and repeat until the washer is emptied. (I recommend you do this with a partner.) Write down how many gallons of water your washer holds.

A chart appears on the next page that gives the amounts of dyebath ingredients for some common sizes of washing machine loads.

If the amount of water for your washing machine load is not on the chart, you will have to calculate your dyebath ingredients as was done in Chapter 7. First, find out the maximum amount of fabric you can dye in your machine. Using the information from the section on Water in Chapter 7, determine the weight of the water by converting the number of gallons to pounds by multiplying by 8. (One gallon of water weighs 8 lbs.) Using the 20:1 water to fabric ratio, divide the weight of the water by 20. This is the weight (in pounds) of the amount of fabric you can dye in your washer.

Example Your washer holds 15 gallons of water. 15 gallons of water weighs 120 pounds (15 x 8). Divide 120 by 20. You can dye up to 6 pounds of fabric in your washer. Calculate your dyebath ingredient amounts for 6 pounds of fabric, even if you are dyeing less.

CHART 8

Washing Machine Dyebath Ingredients

CHART 8: WASHING MACHINE DYEBATH INGREDIENTS				
WATER	**FABRIC**	**SALT**	**SODA**	**DYE** (4%owg)
18 gal	7 lb	7 lb	11.5 oz	4.5 oz
24 gal	9.5 lb	9.5 lb	15 oz	6 oz
30 gal	12 lb	12 lb	19 oz	7.5 oz
36 gal	14.5 lb	14.5 lb	23 oz	9 oz
42 gal	17 lb	17 lb	27 oz	11 oz
46 gal	18.5 lb	18.5 lb	29 oz	12 oz

Now use Chapter 7 to calculate the remaining dyebath ingredients.

When you are ready to begin dyeing, fill up the washing machine with warm water. Turn the machine off. Remove and set aside the water you are using to dissolve the dye.

From this point on, the washer will do most of the work. Add the salt, water softener if you are using it, and dissolved dye. Turn the washer back on and let it agitate a minute or so. Stop it and add the dampened fabric.

Let the washer agitate for 5 minutes. Turn it off and let the fabric soak for 10 minutes. Do this again: 5 minute agitation, 10 minutes soak ("5 & 10"). You may need to reset your machine cycle at the beginning of each 5 minute agitation. Do not let any of your dyebath escape by mistake!

At the end of the second "5 & 10," add the dissolved soda ash. If your fabric is too heavy and sloppy to remove, add the dissolved soda ash in 3 installments. Push the fabric to one side of the washer and add one-third of the dissolved soda ash. Use the bleach port if your washing machine has one. Turn the machine back on and let it agitate for 3 minutes. Repeat twice more.

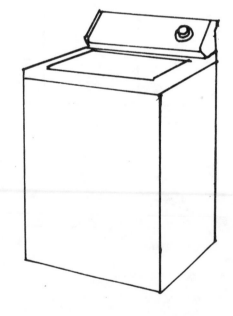

Do 4 more "5 & 10"s. Let the washing machine finish the cycle after the last one. Add Synthrapol to the washer and run a full cycle with hot water to scour the fabric.

CHAPTER 20.

Additional Project Sheets

This chapter contains additional project sheets, similar to the ones found earlier in this book. To do these projects, you need these dyes: PRO Blue 404, Red MX-5B, Yellow MX-4G, PRO Black 602, and Black MX-CWA. Here is a directory to these projects:

Project #9:   Simple Color Gradation   (PRO Blue 404)

Project #10: Simple Color Gradation   (Red MX-5B)

Project #11: Simple Color Gradation   (Yellow MX-4G)

Project #12: Simple Color Gradation   (PRO Black 602)

Project #13: Simple Two Color Gradation   (Red MX-5B, Black 602)

Project #14: Simple Two Color Gradation   (Yellow MX-4G, Black MX-CWA)

Project #15: Simple Two Color Gradation   (Yellow MX-4G, Black 602)

Project #16: Simple Two Color Gradation   (PRO Blue 404, Black MX-CWA)

Project #17: Simple Two Color Gradation   (PRO Blue 404, Black 602)

Project #18: Gradation with a Constant   (PRO Blue 404, Red MX-5B)

Project #19: Same Quantity Gradation   (PRO Blue 404, Yellow MX-G)

Project #20: One Up, One Down Gradation   (Yellow MX-4G, Red MX-5B)

PROJECT #9:

Simple Color Gradation Series

Fabric: 1/2 yd Quilt-cotton per dyepot   (Total: 3 yards)

Measuring Equipment: 6 dyepots, 12 8-oz plastic containers, one beaker, a two cup measure, and one set of measuring spoons. See Chapter 6 for the remaining equipment.

Dye Needed: PRO Blue 404   (Class III)

1. 2 C PRO Blue 404   (8%owf)

2. 1 C PRO Blue 404   (4%owf)

3. 1/2 C PRO Blue 404   (2%owf)

4. 1/4 C PRO Blue 404   (1%owf)

5. 1/8 C PRO Blue 404   (0.5%owf)

6. 1/16 C PRO Blue 404   (0.25%owf)

Measure **cups of concentrate** into the above dyepots.

Preparation

Dyepots: Put in each dyepot: 3 T salt
1 tsp water softener (only if needed)
2 C warm water

Concentrate: Mix: 3 tsp PRO Blue 404 in 4 C warm water

Measurement: : Do a Simple Color Gradation Series. (See Project #4.)

Alkali: Dissolve for each dyepot: 2-1/4 tsp soda ash in 1 C **hot** water.

PROJECT #10:

Simple Color Gradation Series

Fabric: 1/2 yd Quilt-cotton per dyepot   (Total: 3 yards)

Measuring Equipment: 6 dyepots, 12 8-oz plastic containers, one beaker, a two cup measure, and one set of measuring spoons. See Chapter 6 for the remaining equipment.

Dye Needed: Red MX-5B   (Class III)

1.	2 C Red MX-5B	(8%owf)
2.	1 C Red MX-5B	(4%owf)
3.	1/2 C Red MX-5B	(2%owf)
4.	1/4 C Red MX-5B	(1%owf)
5.	1/8 C Red MX-5B	(0.5%owf)
6.	1/16 C Red MX-5B	(0.25%owf)

Measure **cups of concentrate** into the above dyepots.

Preparation

Dyepots: Put in each dyepot: 3 T salt
1 tsp water softener (only if needed)
2 C warm water

Concentrate: Mix: 3 tsp Red MX-5B in 4 C warm water

Measurement: Do a Simple Color Gradation Series. (See Project #4.)

Alkali: Dissolve for each dyepot: 2-1/4 tsp soda ash in 1 C **hot** water.

PROJECT #11:

Simple Color Gradation Series

Fabric: 1/2 yd Quilt-cotton per dyepot   (Total: 3 yards)

Measuring Equipment: 6 dyepots, 12 8-oz plastic containers, one beaker, a two cup measure, and one set of measuring spoons. See Chapter 6 for the remaining equipment.

Dye Needed: Yellow MX-4G   (Class II)

1. 2 C Yellow MX-4G   (4%owf)

2. 1 C Yellow MX-4G   (2%owf)

3. 1/2 C Yellow MX-4G   (1%owf)

4. 1/4 C Yellow MX-4G   (0.5%owf)

5. 1/8 C Yellow MX-4G   (0.25%owf)

6. 1/16 C Yellow MX-4G   (0.125%owf)

Measure **cups of concentrate** into the above dyepots.

Preparation

Dyepots: Put in each dyepot: 3 T salt
                                         1 tsp water softener (only if needed)
                                         2 C warm water

Concentrate: Mix: 1-1/4 Yellow MX-4G in 4 C warm water

  Note: Yellow MX-4G has its maximum color strength at 4%owf. The mixture above is actually 2 cups of Basic Concentrate with 2 additional cups of water to do the gradation.
Measurement: Do a Simple Color Gradation Series. (See Project #4.)

Alkali: Dissolve for each dyepot: 2-1/4 tsp soda ash in 1 C **hot** water.

PROJECT #12:

Simple Color Gradation Series

Fabric: 1/2 yd Quilt-cotton per dyepot   (Total: 3 yards)

Measuring Equipment: 6 dyepots, 12 8-oz plastic containers, one beaker, a two cup measure, and one set of measuring spoons. See Chapter 6 for the remaining equipment.

Dye Needed: PRO Black 602   (Class IV)

1. 2 C Black 602   (10%owf)

2. 1 C Black 602   (5%owf)

3. 1/2 C Black 602   (2.5%owf)

4. 1/4 C Black 602   (1.25%owf)

5. 1/8 C Black 602   (0.63%owf)

6. 1/16 C Black 602   (0.32%owf)

Measure **cups of concentrate** into the above dyepots.

Preparation

Dyepots: Put in each dyepot: 3 T salt
                                   1 tsp water softener (only if needed)
                                   2 C warm water

Concentrate: Mix: 4-1/2 tsp PRO Black 602 in 4 C warm water

Note: PRO Black 602 reachs its maximum color strength at a 10%owf solution.

Measurement: Do a Simple Color Gradation Series. (See Project #4.)

Alkali: Dissolve for each dyepot: 2-1/4 tsp soda ash in 1 C **hot** water.

PROJECT #13:

Simple Two Color Gradation Series

Fabric: 1/2 yd Quilt-cotton per dyepot   (Total: 3 yards)

Measuring Equipment: 6 dyepots, 12 8-oz plastic containers, one beaker, a two cup measure, and one set of measuring spoons. See Chapter 6 for the remaining equipment.

Dyes Needed: PRO Black 602   (Class IV)
                          Red MX-5B   (Class III)

1. 1 C PRO Black 602	1 C Red MX-5B	(8%owf, combined)
2. 1/2 C Black	1/2 C Red	(4%owf, combined)
3. 1/4 C Black	1/4 C Red	(2%owf, combined)
4. 1/8 C Black	1/8 C Red	(1%owf, combined)
5. 1/16 C Black	1/16 C Red	(0.5%owf, combined)
6. 1/32 C Black	1/32 C Red	(0.25%owf, combined)

Measure **cups of concentrate** into the above dyepots.

Preparation

Dyepots: Put in each dyepot: 3 T salt
                                     1 tsp water softener (only if needed)
                                     2 C warm water

Concentrate: Mix: 2 C PRO Black 602   (1-3/4 tsp dye: 2 C water)
                          2 C Red MX-5B   (1-1/2 tsp dye: 2 C water)

Mix concentrates together in one 4 C beaker or pitcher.

Measurement: Do a Simple Two Color Gradation Series. (See Project #5.)

Alkali: Dissolve for each dyepot: 2-1/4 tsp soda ash in 1 C **hot** water.

PROJECT #14:

Simple Two Color Gradation Series

Fabric: 1/2 yd Quilt-cotton per dyepot   (Total: 3 yards)

Measuring Equipment: 6 dyepots, 12 8-oz plastic containers, one beaker, a two cup measure, and one set of measuring spoons. See Chapter 6 for the remaining equipment.

Dyes Needed: Black MX-CWA   (Class III)
                       Yellow MX-4G   (Class II)

1. 1 C Black MX-CWA	1 C Yellow MX-4G	(8%owf, combined)
2. 1/2 C Black	1/2 C Yellow	(4%owf, combined)
3. 1/4 C Black	1/4 C Yellow	(2%owf, combined)
4. 1/8 C Black	1/8 C Yellow	(1%owf, combined)
5. 1/16 C Black	1/16 C Yellow	(0.5%owf, combined)
6. 1/32 C Black	1/32 C Yellow	(0.25%owf, combined)

Measure **cups of concentrate** into the above dyepots.

Preparation

Dyepots: Put in each dyepot: 3 T salt
                                       1 tsp water softener (only if needed)
                                       2 C warm water

Concentrate: Mix: 2 C Black MX-CWA   (1-1/2 tsp dye: 2 C water)
                       2 C Yellow MX-4G   (1-1/4 tsp dye: 2 C water)
Mix concentrates together in one 4 C beaker or pitcher.

Measurement: Do a Simple Two Color Gradation Series. (See Project #5.)

Alkali: Dissolve for each dyepot: 2-1/4 tsp soda ash in 1 C **hot** water

PROJECT #15:

Simple Two Color Gradation Series

Fabric: 1/2 yd Quilt-cotton per dyepot   (Total: 3 yards)

Measuring Equipment: 6 dyepots, 12 8-oz plastic containers, one beaker, a two cup measure, and one set of measuring spoons. See Chapter 6 for the remaining equipment.

Dyes Needed: PRO Black 602   (Class IV)
                          Yellow MX-4G   (Class II)

1. 1 C PRO Black 602	1 C Yellow MX-4G	(8%owf, combined)
2. 1/2 C Black	1/2 C Yellow	(4%owf, combined)
3. 1/4 C Black	1/4 C Yellow	(2%owf, combined)
4. 1/8 C Black	1/8 C Yellow	(1%owf, combined)
5. 1/16 C Black	1/16 C Yellow	(0.5%owf, combined)
6. 1/32 C Black	1/32 C Yellow	(0.25%owf, combined)

Measure **cups of concentrate** into the above dyepots.

Preparation

Dyepots: Put in each dyepot: 3 T salt
                                          1 tsp water softener (only if needed)
                                          2 C warm water

Concentrate: Mix: 2 C PRO Black 602   (1-3/4 tsp dye: 2 C water)
                          2 C Yellow MX-4G (1-1/4 tsp dye: 2 C water)

Mix concentrates together in one 4 C beaker or pitcher.

Measurement: Do a Simple Two Color Gradation Series. (See Project #5.)

Alkali: Dissolve for each dyepot: 2-1/4 tsp soda ash in 1 C **hot** water.

PROJECT #16:

Simple Two Color Gradation Series

Fabric: 1/2 yd Quilt-cotton per dyepot   (Total: 3 yards)

Measuring Equipment: 6 dyepots, 12 8-oz plastic containers, one beaker, a two cup measure, and one set of measuring spoons. See Chapter 6 for the remaining equipment.

Dyes Needed: Black MX-CWA   (Class III)
                     PRO Blue 404   (Class III)

1. 1 C Black MX-CWA	1 C PRO Blue 404	(8%owf, combined)
2. 1/2 C Black	1/2 C Blue	(4%owf, combined)
3. 1/4 C Black	1/4 C Blue	(2%owf, combined)
4. 1/8 C Black	1/8 C Blue	(1%owf, combined)
5. 1/16 C Black	1/16 C Blue	(0.5%owf, combined)
6. 1/32 C Black	1/32 C Blue	(0.25%owf, combined)

Measure **cups of concentrate** into the above dyepots.

Preparation

Dyepots: Put in each dyepot: 3 T salt
                               1 tsp water softener (only if needed)
                               2 C warm water

Concentrate: Mix: 2 C Black MX-CWA   (1-1/2 tsp dye: 2 C water)
                        2 C PRO Blue 404   (1-1/2 tsp dye: 2 C water)

Mix concentrates together in one 4 C beaker or pitcher.

Measurement: Do a Simple Two Color Gradation Series. (See Project #5.)

Alkali: Dissolve for each dyepot: 2-1/4 tsp soda ash in 1 C **hot** water.

PROJECT #17:

Simple Two Color Gradation Series

Fabric: 1/2 yd Quilt-cotton per dyepot   (Total: 3 yards)

Measuring Equipment: 6 dyepots, 12 8-oz plastic containers, one beaker, a two cup measure, and one set of measuring spoons. See Chapter 6 for the remaining equipment.

Dyes Needed: PRO Black 602   (Class IV)
                     PRO Blue 404   (Class III)

1. 1 C PRO Black 602	1 C PRO Blue 404	(8%owf, combined)
2. 1/2 C Black	1/2 C Blue	(4%owf, combined)
3. 1/4 C Black	1/4 C Blue	(2%owf, combined)
4. 1/8 C Black	1/8 C Blue	(1%owf, combined)
5. 1/16 C Black	1/16 C Blue	(0.5%owf, combined)
6. 1/32 C Black	1/32 C Blue	(0.25%owf, combined)

Measure **cups of concentrate** into the above dyepots.

Preparation

Dyepots: Put in each dyepot: 3 T salt
                                     1 tsp water softener (only if needed)
                                     2 C warm water

Concentrate: Mix: 2 C PRO Black 602 (1-3/4 tsp dye: 2 C water)
                        2 C PRO Blue 404   (1-1/2 tsp dye: 2 C water)

Mix concentrates together in one 4 C beaker or pitcher.

Measurement: Do a Simple Two Color Gradation Series. (See Project #5.)

Alkali: Dissolve for each dyepot: 2-1/4 tsp soda ash in 1 C **hot** water.

PROJECT #18:

Color Gradation with a Constant

Fabric: 1/2 yd Quilt-cotton per dyepot   (Total: 3 yards)

Measuring Equipment: 6 dyepots, 12 8-oz plastic containers, two beaker, a two cup measure, and one set of measuring spoons. See Chapter 6 for the remaining equipment.

Dyes Needed: PRO Blue 404   (Class III)
                      Red MX-5B   (Class III)

1. 1 C Red MX-5B   1/2 C PRO Blue 404

2. 1/2 C Red   1/2 C Blue

3. 1/4 C Red   1/2 C Blue

4. 1/8 C Red   1/2 C Blue

5. 1/16 C Red   1/2 C Blue

6. 1/32 C Red   1/2 C Blue

Measure **cups of concentrate** into the above dyepots.

Preparation

Dyepots: Put in dyepots: 3 T salt
                                1 tsp water softener (only if needed)
                                2 C warm water

Concentrate: Mix: 3 C PRO Blue 404   (2-1/4 tsp dye : 3 C warm water)
                         2 C Red MX-5B   (1-1/2 tsp dye : 2 C warm water)

Measurement: Do a Gradation with a Constant. (See Project #6.)

Alkali: Dissolve for each dyepot: 2-1/4 tsp soda ash in 1 C hot water.

PROJECT #19:

Same Quantity Gradation

Fabric: 1/2 yd Quilt-cotton per dyepot   (Total: 2-1/2 yards)

Measuring Equipment: 5 dyepots, 10 8-oz plastic containers, 2 beakers, a two cup measure, and one set of measuring spoons. See Chapter 6 for the remaining equipment.

Dyes Needed: PRO Blue 404   (Class III)
                         Yellow MX-4G   (Class II)

1. 1 C Yellow MX-4G   ------------------

2. 3/4 C Yellow   1/4 C PRO Blue 404

3. 1/2 C Yellow   1/2 C Blue

4. 1/4 C Yellow   3/4 C Blue

5. ------------------- 1 C Blue

Measure **cups of concentrate** into the above dyepots.

Preparation

Dyepots: Put in dyepots: 3 T salt
                                  1 tsp water softener (only if needed)
                                  2 C warm water

Concentrate: Mix: 2-1/2 C PRO Blue 404   (1-7/8 tsp dye : 2-1/2 C warm water)
                          3 C Yellow MX-4G   (1-7/8 tsp dye : 3 C warm water)

(There will be 1/2 C leftover yellow concentrate.)

Measurement: Do a Same Quantity Gradation (See Project #7).

Alkali: Dissolve for each dyepot: 2-1/4 tsp soda ash in 1 C **hot** water.

PROJECT #20:

One Up, One Down Gradation

Fabric: 1/2 yd Quilt-cotton per dyepot   (Total: 6 yards)

Measuring Equipment: 6 dyepots, 12 8-oz plastic containers, 2 beakers, 1 two cup measure, 1 set of measuring spoons, 1 set of measuring cups. See Chapter 6 for the remaining equipment.

Dyes Needed: Yellow MX-4G   (Class II)
                     Red MX-5B   (Class III)

1. 1 C Red MX-5B   ------------------

2. 1/2 C Red   1/16 C Yellow MX-4G

3. 1/4 C Red   1/8 C Yellow

4. 1/8 C Red   1/4 C Yellow

5. 1/16 C Red   1/2 C Yellow

6. ---------------   1 C Yellow

Measure **cups of concentrate** into the above dyepots.

Preparation

Dyepots: Put in dyepots: 3 T salt
                                 1 tsp water softener (only if needed)
                                 2 C warm water

Concentrate: Mix: 2 C Red MX-5B   (1-1/2 tsp dye : 2 C warm water)
                        2 C Yellow MX-4G   (1-1/4 tsp dye : 2 C warm water)

Measurement: Do a One Up, One Down Gradation (See Project #8).

Alkali: Dissolve for each dyepot: 2-1/4 tsp soda ash in 1 C **hot** water.

CHAPTER 21.

Abbreviations & Equivalencies

Abbreviations

ml.....milliliter   C...........cup
tsp....teaspoon   pt...........pint
gm...........gram   qt..........quart
T....tablespoon   gal........gallon
oz........ounce   lb........pound
     cc..........cubic centimeter

Fraction review

7/8 = 1/2 + 1/4 + 1/8
3/4 = 1/2 + 1/4
5/8 = 1/2 + 1/8
3/8 = 1/4 + 1/8

Equivalencies

3 teaspoons = 1 tablespoon
1 pint = 2 cups
1 quart = 2 pints = 4 cups
1 gallon = 4 quarts = 8 pints = 32 cups

1 pound of salt measures 1-1/2 cups.
1 cup of salt weighs 10 oz.

1/16 C water measures 15 ml, or 15 cc.
1/32 C water measures 7.5 ml, or 7.5 cc.
1/64 C water measures 3.8 ml, or 3.8 cc.
1/128 C water measures 1.4 ml, or 1.4 cc.

4%owf solution produces a dark hue.
2%owf solution produces a medium hue.
1%owf solution produces a medium/light hue.
0.5%owf solution produces a light hue.
0.25%owf solution produces a very light hue.
0.125%owf solution produces a pale hue.

1 cup of Basic Concentrate
     contains a 4%owf solution of dye.
1/2 cup of Basic Concentrate
     contains a 2%owf solution of dye.
1/4 cup of Basic Concentrate
     contains a 1%owf solution of dye.
1/8 cup of Basic Concentrate
     contains a 0.5%owf solution of dye.
1/16 cup of Basic Concentrate
     contains a 0.25%owf solution of dye.

1 gallon of water weighs
     8 lbs, or 128 oz, or 3629 gms.
1 quart of water weighs
     2 lbs, or 32 oz, or 907.25 gms.
1 cup   of water weighs
     0.5 lb, or 8 oz, or 227 gms.

1 tablespoon of soda ash weighs 9 gms.
1 teaspoon of dye weighs 3 gms (on the average).

CHAPTER 22.

Dye Color Comparison Chart

BROOKS & FLYNN	PRO CHEMICAL	FABDEC	CERULEAN BLUE
#1 Lemon Yellow MX-8G	Yellow 108 MX-8G	Brilliant Yellow MX-8G	Brilliant Yellow MX-8G
#2 Bright Yellow MX-4G	Yellow 114 MX-4G	Yellow MX-4G	Lemon Yellow MX-4G
#3 Golden Yellow MX-GR	Yellow 112 MX-GR		
#4 Deep Yellow MX-3RA	Yellow 104 MX-3RA		Gold Yellow MX-3RA
#5 Soft Yellow MX-G		Orange MX-G	
#6 Deep Orange MX-2R	Orange 202 MX-2R		
#7 Burnt Orange MX-GRN	Brown 515 MX-GRN	Rust Brown MX-GRN	Rust MX-GRN
#9 Scarlet MX-BRA	Scarlet 300 MX-BRA	Scarlet MX-BRA	
			Bright Scarlet MX-BA
#10 Fire Red MX-BA	Red 310 MX-BA		Carmine Red MX-BA
#10A Chinese Red MX-GBA	Red 312 MX-GBA		
#11A Rose Red MX-G 200%		Warm Red MX-G	
#12 Light Red MX-5B	Red 305 MX-5B		
#13 Fuchsia Red MX-8B	Red 308 MX-8B	Cool Red MX-8B	Fuchsia MX-8B
#19 Plum MX-3R			
	Burgundy 316 MX-6BDA		
#22 Cobalt Blue MX-2GA 150%	Blue 402c MX-2GA 150%	Navy MX-2GA	Navy MX-2GA 150%
#23 Cerulean Blue MX-G, conc.	Blue 406 MX-G, conc.	Brilliant Blue MX-G, conc.	Cerulean Blue MX-G
#24 Navy Blue MX-2RDA	Blue 415 MX-2RDA		Prussian Blue MX-2RDA

113

BROOKS & FLYNN	PRO CHEMICAL	FABDEC	CERULEAN BLUE
#25 Turquoise MX-G	Turquoise 410 MX-G	Turquoise MX-G	Turquoise MX-G
#26 Sky Blue MX-R	Blue 400 MX-R	Blue MX-R	Brilliant Blue MX-R
	Navy 420c MX-RB 150%		Midnight Blue MX-RB
#28 Blue Green MX-CBA	Green 700 MX-CBA		
#36 Maroon Brown MX-5BR	Brown 505 MX-5BR	Red Brown MX-5BR	Red Brown MX-5BR
	Brown 511 MX-RDA		
#39 Black MX-CWA	Black 600 MX-CWA	Black MX-CWA	Black MX-CWA
#44 Better Black	Black 602		

All of the above dye houses are distributers of ICI manufactured dye. Some (i.e. PRO Chemical & Dye, Co, Brooks & Flynn) also blend their own dyes, using ICI chemicals.

This chart only shows the standard ICI colors carries by these major dye houses. Each house names the colors; the MX number is not changed. This can be very confusing! For example, #7 Burnt Orange, Brown 515, Rust Brown, and Rust are all the same color-which is about the hue of butterscotch!

This is by no means all the colors of Procion MX dye available. Brooks & Flynn carry 67 lab-blended colors. PRO Chemical and Dye, Co. has 21 additional lab-blended colors. This makes a total of 115 hues available!

CHAPTER 23.

Suppliers

BROOKS & FLYNN, P.O. Box 2639, Rohnert Park, CA   94927. 1-800-822-2372
(in CA, 1-800-345-2026)
70 hues of Procion MX, and more. Free catalog with color chart.

CERULEAN BLUE, LTD., P.O. Box 21168, Seattle, WA 98111-3168. 206-443-7744.
A dyer's department store! 16 shades of Procion MX series dyes, books, fabrics, 18"
rubber gloves, beakers, and much more. The very informative catalog contains a
color chart and is $4.50.

EARTH GUILD, One Tingle Alley, Asheville, NC 28801. 1-800-327-8448
14 shades of Procion MX series dyes, books, and much more. Catalog is $2, refundable
with your first order.

FABDEC, 3553 Old Post Rd, San Angelo, TX 76904. 915-944-1031
15 shades of Procion MX dyes, fabrics.

PRO CHEMICAL & DYE, INC., P.O. Box 14, Somerset, MA   02726. 617-676-3838.
37 hues of Procion MX dyes, long gloves, plastic beakers and syringes, hand cleaner,
and much more. Free catalog with color chart. They give free technical assistance and
are very helpful.

RUPERT, SPIDER & GIBBON, 718 College St, Healdsburg, CA 95448. 707-433-9577.
High quality silks and cottons for dyeing and much more. Send long SASE for
catalog.

SHADES, 2880 Holcomb Br. Rd., Suite 13-9, Alpharetta, GA 30201. 404-587-1706.
20 (or more) shades of Procion MX dyes, cotton broadcloth, dyeing kits, and other
dyes and equipment. Hand dyed cottons and silks. Brochure is free, fabric swatch set
is $5.

TESTFABRICS, P.O. Drawer 0, 200 Blackford Ave, Middlesex, NJ 08846. 201-469-6446.
This company exclusively carries fabrics that have been prepared for dyeing. Their
fabric sample books are $7 each. Price list is free.

THAI SILKS, 252 State St, Los Altos, CA. 94022. 1-800-845-SILK; in CA, 1-800-345-SILK
Wide selection of high quality white & natural silks suitable for dyeing. Free catalog.

CHAPTER 24.

Bibliography

I. Dyeing

Johnston, Meda Parker and Glen Kaufman. **Design on Fabrics**. Van Nostrand Reinhold, NY, 1967.

Knutson, Linda. **Synthetic Dyes for Natural Fibers**. Rev. Ed. Interweave Press, Loveland, CO, 1986.
    How to use the metric system with fiber-reactive and acid dyes, and more.

Proctor, Richard and Jennifer Lew. **Surface Design for Fabrics**. University of Washington Press, WA, 1984.

Vinroot, Sally and Jeannie Crowder. **The New Dyer**. Interweave Press, Inc., Loveland, CO, 1981. Spiral bound.
    How to use the metric system with fiber reactive, disperse, and acid dyes, and more.

II. Color Theory

Albers, Josef. **Interaction of Color**. Yale University Press, New Haven, CT, 1972.
    The text is available in paperback, but go to a library to examine the original limited edition portfolio with the silkscreened illustrations.

Birren, Faber. **Principles of Color: A Review of Past Traditions and Modern Theories of Color Harmony**. Van Nostrand Reinhold, NY, 1969.

Itten, Johannes. **The Elements of Color**. Edited by Faber Birren. Van Nostrand Reinhold, NY, 1970.

Munsell, Albert H. **A Grammar of Color**. Edited by Faber Birren. Van Nostrand Reinhold, NY, 1969.

III. Color Mixing

Hickethier, Alfred. **Color Mixing by Numbers**. Van Nostrand Reinhold, NY, 1969.
    Plastic binding, sold wrapped.

Kueppers, Harold. **Color Atlas: A Practical Guide for Color Mixing**. Barrons, Woodbury, NY, 1982.

Stockton, James. **Designers Guide to Color**. Books 1 & 2. Chronicle Books, San Francisco, CA, 1984.

CHAPTER 25.

Glossary

"Adjusted Basic Concentrate". A Basic Concentrate which uses some amount of dye other than 4%owf in a one cup quantity.

Adsorption. The way in which the dye molecules are assimilated onto the surface of the fabric by the suppression of the negative surface charges of the fabric during the first phase of dyeing.

"Basic Concentrate". A Basic Concentrate is a dye concentrate that is mixed according to this guideline: one cup of Basic Concentrate contains enough dye (usually defined as 4% of the weight of the fabric) of that color for less than one pound of fabric at a 20:1 water to fiber ratio. When working with one pound or more of fabric, two cups of Basic Concentrate contains a solution with an amount of dye that is 4% of the weight of the fabric. For example, two cups of Basic Concentrate for dyeing one pound of fabric would contain 18.16 gms (rounded off to 18 grams) of dye.

Basic Concentrates are used as aids in color mixing, planning sheet writing, and color recipe recording. See Chapter 9.

Chemical Water. A mixture of urea and water (9 T Urea to 1 qt water). Used in mixing dye paint for direct application of dye, as in tie dyeing. See Chapter 18.

Chroma. A term describing the brightness, intensity, or degree of saturation of a color.

Color Recipe. A description for dyeing a particular color. See Chapter 12.

Color Wheel. An array of colors showing the primaries, secondaries, and intermediate colors.

Complementary Colors. Colors opposite each other on the color wheel. Mixing these produces browns and grays.

Dye. An agent for coloring or staining. They can be either natural or synthetic. Synthetic dyes include: acid dyes (for wool and silk), disperse dyes (for synthetic fabrics), direct dyes (for cellulose fibers), and fiber reactive dyes (for cellulose fibers and silks). Household or Union dyes contain a combination of the above dye types. Procion MX series dyes are fiber reactive dyes.

Dye Concentrate. A preparation of dye and water that is added to the dyebath. They can be mixed for each dyebath, or collectively as Basic Concentrates. See Chapter 8, 9.

Dye Session. The period of time when fabric is dyed.

Dyepot. The container in which fabric is dyed. It can be plastic, enamel, glass, or stainless steel. See Chapter 6.

Dyebath. The solution of dye, water, salt, and other assisting agents in which fabric is dyed. See Chapter 7.

Discharge Dyeing. The use of bleach or other stripping agents to remove color from fabric. See Chapter 18.

Exhaust Dyeing. During exhaust dyeing, the color potential of the dyestuff is completely spent at the end of the dye session. This book uses a method of exhaust dyeing with Procion MX dyes. See Long Dye Bath.

Fiber Reactive Dye. With a fiber reactive dye, the dye chemically reacts with the fiber, using salt and an alkali such as soda ash as assistants. Procion MX dyes are fiber reactive.

Gradation Series. A series of dyebaths done in a sequence so the colors gradate in hue or value. See Chapter 15.

Hue. Another word for color.

Hydrolization. The reacting of the dyestuff with water.

Intermediate Colors. Colors that lie between a primary and a secondary on a color wheel.

Long Dye Bath Method. An immersion dyeing technique where the dye and fabric have contact with each other in water for a long period of time (one and one half hours). See Exhaust Dyeing.

Measuring Chamber. A enclosed box or space for measuring powdered dye. See Chapter 4.

"Mystery Bucket," "Mystery Fabric." Leftover dissolved dye or concentrates are placed in a separate dyepot, the "Mystery Bucket", to dye "Mystery Fabric." Used by those who cannot bear to throw anything away.

%OWF. An abbreviation for "percentage of weight of fabric." Used to describe the amount of dye used in a particular dyeing situation.

PH. A measuring range for the acidity or alkalinity of a liquid. Liquids with a high pH are more alkaline; those with a low are more acid.

Planning Sheets. These sheets record the information needed for a dye session and serve as a guide during it. See Chapter 12 and the sample projects in the book.

Primary Colors. Colors that cannot be produced through color mixing. There are different types of primaries, depending on the medium being used and the color theory held.

"Quilt-cotton." A medium weight fabric commonly used in quiltmaking. It standardly weighs up at four yards to the pound. Most muslins fall into this category.

"Replacement Water." The water that is added to the measurement beaker during a gradation series to keep the water amount constant. See Chapter 15.

Scouring. The act of washing fabric either prior to dyeing or after it is dyed. Prescouring removes residual chemicals from the fabric. Post-scouring removes salt and hydrolyzed dye. See Chapter 10.

Secondary Colors. Colors produced by mixing pairs of primary colors together.

Shade. A hue or color that has been darkened by mixing with gray, black, brown, or its complement.

Short Dyebath Method. A direct application method of dyeing where dye concentrates are painted, sprayed, etc. onto the fabric which has been treated with an alkali solution. The discussion of tie dyeing in Chapter 18 describes this dye method.

Soda Ash. An alkali substance, sodium carbonate, used as a chemical assist during dyeing. It raises the pH of the water which allows the dye to react chemically with the fiber.

Sodium Carbonate. See Soda Ash.

Synthrapol. A commercial scouring agent.

Tertiary Colors. Colors that contain all three primaries. These are always shades.

Tint. A color that has been lightened by diluting the dye strength with water.

Urea. Used as a moisture retaining agent in direct application (as in tie dyeing or the short bath method) of Procion MX dyes.

Value. The amount of lightness or darkness of a color.

Washing Soda. This is another name for Soda Ash. The washing soda that is commonly sold in the grocery store often contains bleach, making it unsuitable for use in dyeing. See Soda Ash.

Water Weight to Fiber Weight Ratio. The proportion of the amount of water weight to the amount of fiber weight that is optimum for dyeing. When dyeing fabric with Procion MX dyes, the water weight to fiber weight ratio is 20:1. Water weight is also known as liquor weight.

Index

Abbreviations 112
Adsorption 5,117
Basic Concentrate 37-46,117
    adjusting 70
    charts 45-6
    definition 38
    how to measure 39, 41, 51
    how to use charts 42-3
Bibliography 116
Bleaching fabrics 95
Bleeding 57
Calculating amounts
    Basic Concentrate 47
    dye 36
    salt 20
    soda ash 21-2
    water softener 21
    water 20
Chemical water 94,117
Color mixing 66
Color wheel 60-62-5,117
Color Gradations 67ff
    how to do 67-8
    One Up, One Down
        86-9,111
    Same Quantity
        82-5,110
    Simple 68, 71, 100-3
    Simple Two Color
        74-7, 104-8
    use of replacement water 68
    -with a Constant
        78-81, 109
Color recipe 58, 117
Color theory 59
Colorfast 5. 92
Concentrate, Basic (See Basic
    Concentrate)
Discharge dyeing 95, 117
Distilled water 17
Dye 24-6, 33-4, 117
    characteristics 5, 92-3
    chemistry 5
    color comparison charts 113-4
    concentrates 37-43, 117
    disposal 9
    how to 49-53
    how to (summary) 49
    recommended 12, 60-1, 92
    safety 7f, 92
    safety equipment 7
    "setting" 53

weighing 24
weight classes 25, 44
Dye Color Comparison Chart
    113-4
Dye equipment 10-4
    checklist 10-11
    dyepots 12, 117
    measuring 13
    safety equipment 14
Dyebath 15-22, 117
    dye (See Dye)
    fabrics (See Fabrics)
    Ingredient Formula Summary
        23
    Ingredient Summary for
        Quilt-cotton 19
    reusing dyebaths 34, 92
    salt 12, 18, 21-2, 50, 90
    soda ash 12, 18, 21-2, 52-3, 54
    water 17, 20, 50
    water softener 17, 21, 50
Dyebath by Dyebath Measuring
    Method 33, 35, 51, 62-3,35
Dyeing
    what to wear 7, 9, 14
    area 7-9
    washing machine 96ff
Equivalencies 112
Exhaust dyeing 117
Fabrics 5, 12, 50
    how to code 56
    quilt-cotton 3, 15, 118
    washing (scouring) 15, 53
    sample weights 16
Glossary 117-8
Gradations (See Color
    Gradations)
Hydrolization 6, 50, 93, 118
Measuring chambers 8
Measuring dyes, dye concentrates
    Concentrate Method 39, 53
    Dyebath by Dyebath Method
        33, 51
    how to measure dye
        24, 33-4, 93
    how to measure concentrates
        39-40
Myers-Newbury, Jan 67, 83
"Mystery Bucket" 53, 67, 118
"Mystery Fabric" 53, 118
Overdyeing 54, 94
Planning sheets 56, 118

Quickstart 3, 4, 15, 18, 24
"Quilt-cotton" 3, 15, 18, 118
Rearranging the fabric
    52, 53, 54, 94,
Record keeping 57
"Replacement water" 68, 118
Safety 7-8, 33, 92
Scouring (See Washing)
"Setting" the dye 53
Soda Ash (See Dyebath
    Ingredients)
Sodium bisulfite 95
Sodium carbonate (See Soda Ash)
Suppliers 115
Synthrapol 14, 15, 50
Tie dyeing 94
Troubleshooting 54-5
Washing and drying fabric
    14. 15. 53
Washing machine dyeing 96f
Washing soda (See Soda Ash)
Water softener 12, 17, 21, 50
Water to fiber ratio 17, 118
%owf 24, 118
"5 & 10"s 98
PRO Blue 404 61, 62, 64, 66, 73, 78
    80, 91
PRO Chino 500 61, 78, 91
PRO Black 602 61, 91
B/F #19A Lilac 73, 82, 86, 91
B/F #30 Emerald Green 73, 90, 91
B/F #38 Khaki 61, 78, 91
B/F #44 Better Black 61, 91
Black MX-CWA 61, 71-2, 76, 91
Blue Green MX-CBA 78, 86, 91
Brilliant Yellow MX-8G
    61, 66, 73, 82, 90
Cerulean Blue MX-G 25, 61, 73,78,
    82, 86, 90, 91
Deep Yellow MX-3RA 82, 86, 90
Fuchsia MX-8B 25, 61, 66, 82, 90
Golden Yellow MX-GR 70, 86, 90,
Lemon Yellow MX-4G 61, 62, 64,
    66, 73, 80, 81, 84,
Orange MX-2R 73, 86, 91
Red MX-5B 61, 62, 64, 66, 73, 76,
    84, 90
Turquoise MX-G 25, 61, 66, 82, 90

ABOUT THIS BOOK

Creating Color was produced with the aid of desktop publishing. The manuscript was prepared on an Apple IIc computer using WordPerfect. In order to typeset the text, the manuscript disc was converted to a MasIntosh formatted disc in WordPerfect. The selected typefaces are Palatino and Helvetica. The book design and pen and ink illustrations are done by Judy Anne Walter. The typeset copy of the manuscript was printed on a Laserwriter Plus printer. The cover art was designed by the author and typeset by Davidson Typographers, Inc, Chicago, IL. Color separations and film preparation for the cover were done by Chromalith Color Studio, Inc., Chicago, IL. The book was printed and bound by MacNaughton & Gunn Lithographers in Ann Arbor, MI.

JUDY ANNE WALTER is a fiber artist who works in the areas of both contemporary quiltmaking and knitwear design. Her award winning quilts have been seen in one woman, invitational, and group shows throughout the United States. Her wearable art has toured on five occasions in the prestigous Fairfield/Concord Fashion Shows. Ms. Walter's work is included in private, public, and corporate art collections. Examples of her work have appeared in numerous publications, including the *Fiberarts Design Book III, Quilter's Newsletter Magazine,* and *American Quilter*.

Ms. Walter is also an acclaimed fiberarts instructor, offering workshops on dyeing, fabric painting, surface design, patchwork quilting, and knitting. She was named "1986 Teacher of the Year" by *Professional Quilter Magazine*. She travels nationally to give lectures and workshops for fiber guilds and at quilt conferences. She also participates in the Illinois Art Council's Artist in Education Program.

Ms. Walter resides on the north side of Chicago with her husband.

For more information about Judy Anne Walter's artwork and her workshops, send a SASE to:

Judy Anne Walter
Coolor by the Lake Publications
P.O. Box 6149
Evanston, IL 60204